Das Schloß Hohnstein s. Marten S. Petri-Clauskirche S.

Fürstl. Baumgarten

Hertzog Johann Wilhelms Schlos

Vorder Rathaus

New Rathaus

Der Marckt

Der holtzmarckt

Der Marckt

Heinrichs Bann⸗

Dat alt Rathaus

Fürstl.

Lutzelburger haus

Frawen

Lutzelburgers gartt

PETER WASHINGTON

Bach

EVERYMAN'S LIBRARY—EMI CLASSICS
MUSIC COMPANIONS

THIS IS A BORZOI BOOK

PUBLISHED BY ALFRED A. KNOPF, INC.

ISBN 0-375-40002-8

Front endpaper: Bird's-eye view of Weimar: coloured engraving by
Georg Braun and Franz Hogenberg from *Civitates Orbis Terrarum*,
Cologne (AKG London).
Back endpaper: Plan of the city of Leipzig: engraving published by
Matthaeus Seutter, Augsburg, 1723 (British Library, London:
Maps 186.V.p.115).
Frontispiece: Johann Sebastian Bach: oil painting by Elias Gottlob
Haussmann, 1746 (AKG London: Stadtgeschichtliches Museum,
Leipzig).
Title page: Detail from the original edition of Bach's Canon BWV
1076 (Bildarchiv, Österreichischen Nationalbibliothek, Vienna).

Series General Editor: Michael Rose

Picture research by Helen Ottaway

Typeset in the UK by AccComputing, Castle Cary, Somerset
Printed and bound in Germany by Mohndruck Graphische Betriebe
GmbH, Gütersloh

Contents

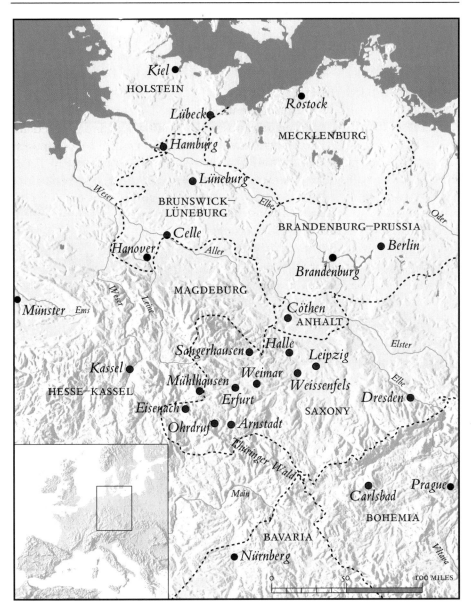

Germany in Bach's Time

Towns indicated in red were lived in or visited by Bach

INTRODUCTION

The Enigma

On 23 April 1843, a monument was unveiled in Leipzig to the memory of a neglected composer who had lived and worked in the town for twenty-seven years until his death in 1750. The composer was Johann Sebastian Bach, and the ceremony was inspired by Felix Mendelssohn and his friend Robert Schumann who recorded the occasion in his magazine, the *Neue Zeitschrift für Musik*. The purpose of the monument was to celebrate Bach's life and draw public attention to his work, but as Schumann noted:

> Honour was paid not only to Bach but also to his sole surviving grandson, a man of eighty-four, still full of energy, with snow-white hair and expressive features. No one knew of his existence, not even Mendelssohn, who had lived so long in Berlin and, he supposed, had followed every trace of Bach he could discover. Yet his grandson had resided there for over forty years. No information was obtained regarding his circumstances, except that he had filled the office of Capellmeister to the consort of Friedrich Wilhelm III, and enjoys a pension which maintains him in comfort.

The presence of Bach's grandson was appropriate for several reasons, not least as a reminder that the great Johann Sebastian was no lone figure in musical history but one member of an enormous clan which produced many other distinguished composers. But perhaps the most interesting aspect of the affair is that no one involved had recalled the old man's existence until he appeared at the ceremony. His obscurity, one might say, is symbolic of a mystery which has cloaked his grandfather from that time to this. For, despite fame in his own lifetime, and a subsequent revival which has now been in progress for 150 years, Bach remains the least familiar of the very great composers.

This may seem a curious claim to make, considering the intensive research into Bach's life and work during the last two centuries, the hundreds of books and articles about him, the thousands of performances his works receive every year. But how many of us, even among professional musicians, know Bach as thoroughly as we know Mozart or Beethoven? Though many pieces are famous, most of his works – hundreds of cantatas and organ works, and especially the late contrapuntal scores – remain unheard. For every thousand performances of the Brandenburg Concertos there is one of the *Musical Offering* or the *Art of Fugue*. Beethoven's last quartets are popular by comparison. Yet these two masterpieces are among the pinnacles of musical achievement, and without some knowledge of them we can hardly hope to understand their composer.

About the man himself we are also comparatively ignorant. The outlines of Bach's life and career are clear enough, but the details remain obscure. Although there is a great deal of relevant official material to hand – council records, royal correspondence, newspaper articles and so on – few personal documents have survived: just twenty-eight letters from a life of sixty-five years. Nor does he make frequent appearances in contemporary memoirs. The contrast with major composers from the second half of the century says everything. Haydn, Mozart and Beethoven are vividly alive for us from letters and diaries. This has something to do with the greater survival of written records from the later eighteenth century, but it owes far more to social and cultural changes which produced a transformation in the status of artists between the death of Bach in 1750 and the death of Beethoven in 1827. Beethoven was a superstar in his own lifetime, Bach by comparison a provincial craftsman – and, what is more, content to regard himself as such.

The consequence is a paradox. Bach's music is stamped with a powerful and unmistakable character, yet the man who created that music remains elusive. There is a comparison to be made here with Shakespeare. He too manifests a strong personality in his work, yet Shakespeare the man is notoriously hard to place. There are also important differences, of course. Shakespeare seems to come from nowhere, crowning a sudden flowering in poetry and drama. Bach emerged from a rich musical culture and a long line of practising musicians. Shakespeare helped to raise a comparatively new art – the popular theatre – to the greatest heights. Bach's work concludes a tradition. Shakespeare retired from the theatre in middle age; Bach went on working to the end. But the crucial similarity is what counts: we know almost nothing about the inner lives of these two monolithic figures in Western culture. This is all the more frustrating in Bach's case because we *do* know so much about the circumstances in which he lived, and even about his own family, whose amply recorded history stretches back to the sixteenth century. In short, Bach is an enigma, and his canonization as a musical saint over the last 150 years has only served to deepen the mystery in which the enigma is wrapped.

By 1843 a revival was already long overdue. Bach's reputation among connoisseurs had survived his death, and the music itself was carefully studied by his greatest successors, including Mozart and Beethoven, but the general public were aware of him only as a name, and a rather daunting name at that. If his work had been little performed at the end of the eighteenth century, this was partly because rapidly changing fashions had made it seem dated, difficult and obscure, and partly because the conditions which produced it began to disappear even in the composer's own lifetime. He had worked for the two major employers of his age, the church and the aristocracy, but by the time he died both were in decline. The cultural landscape was changing out of all recognition, and the Cantors and *Kapellmeisters* produced in such profusion by the Bach family for two hundred years no longer dominated German musical life.

As if to signal this change, the family tree, so vigorous for so long, began to wither. Bach had many children but they themselves had few descendants. Fifty years after Johann Sebastian's death, a Leipzig musical journal drew attention to the fact that his youngest child, Regina Susanna, was now destitute and called for public funds to support her. A number of famous musicians sprang to her rescue, raising a public subscription to which Beethoven proposed to contribute earnings from one of his own works. The publicity helped to stimulate a nascent renewal of interest in Bach's music. Shortly afterwards, in 1802, Johann Nicolaus Forkel published the first biography of the composer which is still a classic. And in 1829 Mendelssohn – a lifelong devotee – signalled the beginning of a full-scale revival with a centenary performance of the *St Matthew Passion*.

Bach's first biographer,
J. N. Forkel (1749–1818).

That major romantic composers like Mendelssohn and Schumann should lead the rediscovery of Bach is itself highly significant for several reasons, not least because it seems at first sight to be so unlikely. Bach was – and is – often thought of as the antithesis of everything we associate with the romantics. Where they supposedly cultivated freedom, originality, spontaneity and expressiveness, he was said by hostile critics to be monumental, dry, academic and backward-looking. His emphasis on complex contrapuntal forms was especially deplored by people who believed that music should be tuneful and directly appealing. The criticisms were common in his own lifetime, more frequent still in the decades following his death. Even Bach's son, Carl Philipp Emanuel, one of his father's staunchest supporters, concluded that there might be some truth in them.

It is understandable that C. P. E. Bach should have found himself constrained to make such an admission. He was, after all, something of a romantic himself: his own music is delicate, melodic, dramatic, full of feeling and often melancholy, though entirely lacking, it has to be said, in the strength and vigour of his father's work. Nevertheless, with all respect to Carl Philipp Emanuel, the antithesis between Bach and the romantics is false. Bach's music is certainly monumental where monumentality is appropriate, and it does employ complex contrapuntal forms. But it is profoundly expressive. And although deeply rooted in traditional techniques, it has an extraordinary capacity to sound new and fresh. It is also – and this hardly needs saying to modern audiences – just as prolific in memorable tunes and heart-stopping moments as the music of any romantic. Of course some of Bach's work is below par; that is true of any composer. Some of it is difficult, occasionally it is simply routine. But to call him dry or academic or reactionary is a travesty of the truth.

Mendelssohn and Schumann clearly recognized Bach's qualities, and

The Morning Hymn
by T. E. Rosenthal, 1870.
A romantic view of the
Bach family at home as seen
through nineteenth-century
eyes.

they saw that the crude oppositions on which hostile criticism was based – between counterpoint and harmony, formality and spontaneity, tradition and originality – were misconceived. For the greatest music either rises above such oppositions or draws strength from them. Bach's counterpoint is not the opposite of melody. His formality does not exclude spontaneity. His compositions can be both magnificent and charged with deep feeling. It may be observed in passing that Franz Schubert, perhaps the finest melodist Western music has ever produced, took pains in adult life to master counterpoint; so did Schumann. And as Mendelssohn understood, if Bach wrote no operas, he did write the *St Matthew Passion*: there are few master-pieces more moving or more dramatic.

After 1843 the revival rapidly gathered pace. Performances took place. Editions of the scores proliferated. Scholars began to research. Books and articles were written, most notably Philipp Spitta's *Johann Sebastian Bach. His work and influence on the music of Germany* which came out in two volumes in 1873 and 1880. But as this remarkable book shows, restoring Bach's music to its proper place was not a simple task. So rare were performances in the decades immediately following his death, and so great the change in musical aesthetics, that appropriate playing styles had been forgotten. And although some of Bach's scores contain extensive directions to players, others do not even indicate the instruments to be used.

The Bach revival was further complicated in the nineteenth century by the fact that one of the important forces working in its favour was the need for German heroes. Although Germany did not exist as a political entity until Bismarck created a new German empire in 1871, German nationalism was a growing power. And precisely because it could not express itself in political institutions before 1871, this national feeling was articulated largely through cultural means: language and literature, philosophy, history and – above all – music past and present. Once again, the comparison with Shakespeare is relevant. Just as Shakespeare became an English national hero, exalted by poets such as Keats and Coleridge, so Bach was presented by German composers as their own great precursor and progenitor. Looked at from this point of view, Handel's cosmopolitanism – such a powerful force in forging his lasting reputation throughout Europe – was perceived as a weakness. Though he and Bach were acclaimed as the leading German composers from the first half of the eighteenth century, it was observed that only Bach had remained true to his roots, both geographical and musical, never stirring from German soil and (despite his absorption of French and Italian influences) cultivating a distinctively polyphonic style based on that most German of musical forms, the Lutheran chorale.

This is the style celebrated by Wagner in his tribute to the glories of German music, *Die Meistersinger von Nürnberg*. That opera is set in the sixteenth century, of course, not the eighteenth, but Bach – or rather a romantic image of Bach – is the presiding spirit behind it. The two composers might seem to be polar opposites, both as men and as musicians, but it is no accident that their reputations were consolidated in parallel during the nineteenth century, for both were seen as quintessentially Teutonic: expressive, philosophic and national. The musical legacy of this image of Bach can be heard in early recordings, some of which are included on the discs accompanying this volume.

A very different idea of the composer prevails in our own time, shaped by the quest for historical authenticity. Musicians today strive to discover how the music 'really' sounded when it first appeared, by playing it on instruments of the period and re-creating the conventions of

Baroque performance. There is a lot to be said for and against both approaches, the subjective romantic and the objective authentic. Bach's music – like Shakespeare's drama – accommodates both, and will no doubt continue to assimilate other changes in interpretive fashion with equal ease. But while such changes form a fascinating chapter in the wider history of music, they pose perplexing questions for the biographer by raising the thorny problem of what, exactly, is being interpreted when music is performed. Is it the notes on the page? The composer's intentions? The conventions of a particular period? What, in short, is the meaning of Bach's music, and how do musicians determine and convey that meaning?

These questions are almost certainly insoluble, though debate about them can be fruitful. It was precisely out of such debate that the authentic movement emerged. But they need to be mentioned here for one vitally important reason. Despite the popularity of authentic performances, most audiences still subscribe to a romantic aesthetic which holds that the major purpose of art is to express its creator's personality. It is the revelation of that personality which constitutes meaning. Whatever its merits, this aesthetic was not shared by Bach. As a hard-working professional, he understood well enough that music has various functions, but he believed that it was primarily a means of articulating the divine order of the universe and thereby worshipping its creator. Music for Bach was not a personal dialect for communicating individual ideas and feelings, but a universal language like mathematics, disclosing eternal truths.

It is for this reason that our limited knowledge of the composer's life – and, in particular, of his inner being – is comparatively unimportant. So far as the relationship between life and music is concerned, what matters to the biographer is Bach's public existence, not his private life. While not neglecting what is known of his strong, loving and often humorous character, the following pages will therefore be taken up mainly with his working conditions, the musical conventions of his time, his religious creed, and the historical, intellectual and social situation in which he found himself. By such a route we can hope to explore – if not solve – the enigma that is Johann Sebastian Bach.

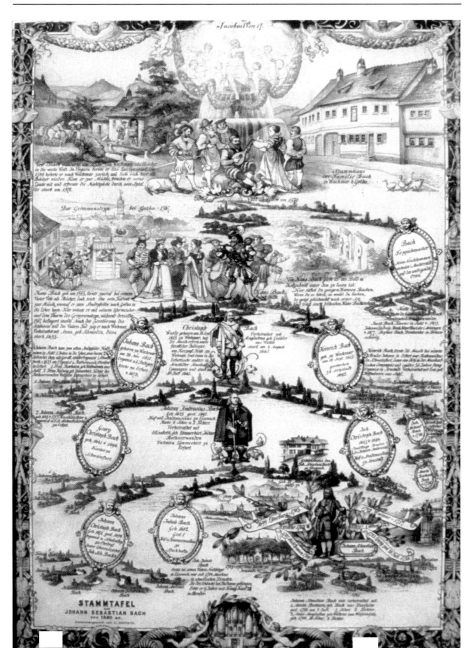

A family tree of the Bach clan, culminating in Johann Sebastian, first published in Germany in the early nineteenth century.

CHAPTER 1

The Background

Everyone is familiar with the dramatic history of Germany in the twentieth century: defeat in two world wars, the horrors of Nazism, the partition of the country in 1949, West Germany's economic miracle in the postwar period and the country's triumphant reunion in 1990. One way or another, the nation's enormous power and its turbulent political history have dominated European politics for over a century, casting long shadows over the rest of the world.

It has not always been so. Until the late nineteenth century, Germany was not one political unit but a vast collection of independent feuding states in all shapes and sizes, more concerned with petty jealousies among themselves than with the world outside. Only in 1871 were these states unified by the king of Prussia's brilliant chancellor, Bismarck, who made his master ruler of a German empire. Even then the regions kept much of their own identity, as indeed they do today. The old kingdoms of Prussia and Saxony, Württemberg and Bavaria, are cultural and social forces to be reckoned with in the republic of the 1990s. The feudal Germany Bach knew still exists under the surface of a modern state.

Though Germany's economic and political pre-eminence within Europe is a comparatively recent phenomenon, German domestic politics have long been a European problem. Straddling the heart of the continent, the territory had been racked with political instability since the Dark Ages when the collapse of the Roman empire left a power vacuum. The Romans had never subdued northern Europe, though they had contained the northern tribes. But as Roman power weakened in the fourth and fifth centuries, these tribes poured south, overwhelming their old enemies with ferocious campaigns of burning, raping and looting which came to a climax in the sack of Rome by Goths in AD 410 and Vandals in AD 455. Twenty-one years later the last Roman emperor in the West was deposed.

For a thousand years after his fall, Europe was in turmoil. Nominally ruled by the pope and the Holy Roman Emperor – who, as his title suggests, laid claim on the one hand to the authority of the Caesars and on the other to the favour of the church – Germany was actually the province of powerful princes. Their hands were strengthened by the fact that the imperial throne was not hereditary. Holy Roman Emperors were appointed by consent of regional overlords who naturally expected to exert influence in return for support. Seven of these overlords – three of them also archbishops – were officially recognized as supreme and their powers formalized: between them they elected the emperor who then struggled to control them. But it was really the seven electors – or at least the most powerful among them – who ruled Germany, either directly or through their influence.

The political situation was complicated by the existence of eighty-eight free imperial cities, in theory answering only to the emperor but in practice virtually independent. Bach worked in one of these cities briefly as a young man, but most of his working life was spent either in provincial towns or in small principalities, such as Anhalt-Cöthen. Some principalities were ancient and powerful. Others – including Anhalt-Cöthen – only existed because of complex inheritance laws which encouraged princely families to divide their estates from time to time. Thus a dukedom might have a main branch and several subsidiaries, each subsidiary controlled by an absolute ruler who owed allegiance only to the head of his own family. If subsidiaries died out, titles and properties reverted to the main branch and the process began again. This inevitably multiplied the number of self-governing states into hundreds and encouraged a constant fluctuation in boundaries and political organizations.

The Protestant Reformation inaugurated by Luther in the early sixteenth century was another complicating factor in the political equation, eventually splitting the German states into two armed camps, Catholics led by the emperor and Protestants led by Lutheran princes. Throughout the sixteenth and seventeenth centuries these two camps struggled for supremacy until they fought each other to a standstill in the Thirty Years' War (1618–48) which drew into the conflict other

European powers including France, Poland and Sweden, devastated large tracts of central Germany and brought plague and famine in its wake. The Treaty of Westphalia which ended the war in 1648 provided for limited religious toleration and the effective separation of church and state. After the treaty was concluded, the Habsburg family, in which the imperial throne had become virtually hereditary, began to lose interest in Germany, preferring to concentrate on its own territories in Austria, Hungary and Bohemia. The consequent power vacuum left the princes free to pursue their own ambitions and the strongest made good use of the opportunity to consolidate and extend their powers.

Broadly speaking, the effect of the Westphalia settlement was to leave southern Germany in Catholic hands while the northern states remained Protestant. The division was to have momentous consequences for Bach who was born in the north and worked there all his life, because it is impossible to separate seventeenth-century European culture from its religious context. Any tourist visiting both northern and southern Germany must be struck by that even today. The very architecture is different. Most of Bach's vocal music was written for the Lutheran Church which dominated northern Germany, and all his organ works were produced for performance in church. More to the point, his whole cultural outlook and musical aesthetic were shaped by Protestant Christianity.

Politically, the result of Westphalia was a kind of controlled chaos, with varying legal and administrative systems, tax laws, currencies, border controls and trading regulations, all compounded by different regional customs and dialects. These differences were exacerbated by despotism. For within their realms, however tiny, German princes were absolute rulers and most were keen to emphasize their independence. Each kept up his court, his government and his army – though it might contain only fifty soldiers – and each insisted on every tittle of respect due to him: lèse-majesté was one of the most severely punished crimes in many German states, on a par with treason. It was not unusual for anyone even suspected of slandering a prince to be thrown in gaol for months without trial, as an example to others.

Even despotism can have its advantages when the ruler is wise, well-disposed and well-advised. In practice, German princes were often stupid, cruel, profligate, selfish, arbitrary and even mad. The worst were monstrous and the best tyrannized over subjects whose main function was to finance the political adventures and building programmes of their masters through taxes imposed without their consent. In return they were controlled by curfews, by-laws and even dress codes which were fiercely enforced.

But there was one artistic advantage to this political system. For an essential aspect of royal life is the display through which a monarch's power is revealed. The hundreds of ruling families therefore competed with one another to create the most beautiful palaces and the most brilliant courts, and though the cost to their subjects was grievous, the cultural results were often remarkable. The great model for these families was the court established by Louis XIV at the end of the seventeenth century in the vast palace he built at Versailles, where the life of his courtiers was governed by a complex system of etiquette and a rigid observance of social hierarchy. Louis had experienced in childhood the horrors of civil war during the aristocratic uprisings known as the Fronde, in which powerful nobles threatened to displace the royal family, and he was determined to control the nobles by compelling them to live under his eye. So the original small château on the site at Versailles was gradually transformed into what amounted to a small town some miles outside Paris, where the entire court could live and be supervised personally by the king.

Louis' life at Versailles was like an elaborate stage performance in which his courtiers served as extras, with an unending series of entertainments to distract them from any interest in politics. This performance required a suitably grand setting: not only a palace with its magnificent fittings in the way of furniture, pictures and sculptures, but also gardens, orangeries, stables, a theatre and a chapel where the monarch could worship the God who had supposedly appointed him. All these establishments had to be staffed with an enormous retinue of servants, from cleaners and gardeners at the bottom of the hierarchy, to major-domos, stewards, composers, painters, sculptors and doctors at the top.

Everyone in Europe was fascinated by Versailles – and everyone of any consequence wanted to visit the palace. The king of Sweden even employed a special ambassador whose only duty was to report on changing artistic fashions at the French court. Royal guests, received by the king himself, were duly impressed by the grandeur of the man who came to be known as *le roi soleil* – the Sun King. They took note of his complete authority over even the grandest of his subjects and the methods he employed to secure that authority; and they realized that Versailles was not merely a means of displaying royal power: it was also a way of maintaining it. For Louis XIV kept a very tight rein on his subjects; and the grander the subject, the tighter the rein. What better way could there be for an absolute ruler to combine pleasure with the establishment of his dictatorship?

Returning from Versailles, every petty German prince was naturally anxious to emulate this paragon. As a matter of honour, each court therefore had to have its library, its museum, its art gallery, its gardens and its chapel. One or two even had theatres. A large staff was required to service these establishments, especially when the prince had a taste for music and kept a court orchestra. There was already a magnificent tradition of German sacred music by composers such as Heinrich Schütz, but the example of Versailles prompted the rapid development of native secular music. The complex cross-fertilization of the two domains – church and court – was to produce a musical culture whose variety and richness were rivalled only in Italy. By the end of the seventeenth century, the time and the conditions were ripe for Germany to produce major composers. As if on cue, two duly appeared, both born in 1685 and within a few miles of each other. One was George Frideric Handel. The other was Johann Sebastian Bach. Between them, they were to define the limits of European music in the first half of the eighteenth century.

*   *   *

*Louis XIV receiving Elector Friedrich August I of Saxony at Fontainebleau
on 27 September 1714. Painting by Louis de Silvestre the elder.*

Lying just south of the Harz mountains, Thuringia is one of the most
beautiful parts of Germany; in the late Middle Ages it was also one of
the most prosperous. Mountainous, wooded and fertile, with rich agricul-
tural land, large mineral deposits and extensive light industry, the region
had suffered badly in the Thirty Years' War which decimated the
population, but by the end of the seventeenth century political conditions
had stabilized and prosperity was returning. Then as now, the area was
traversed by deep forests and dotted with black-and-white market towns.
There are also many castles, most famously the Wartburg, where Martin
Luther sheltered after issuing his challenge to the Catholic authorities
which signalled the onset of the Reformation in 1521, and where he
began his translation of the New Testament.

A few miles north of the Wartburg, in the Thuringian forest, is the
walled town of Eisenach. At the time of Bach's birth Eisenach was rather

more than a country town. Because of dispositions made by the duke of Saxe-Weimar in 1672, a cadet branch of the family had been established as dukes of Saxe-Eisenach, an arrangement which lasted until 1741 when the title lapsed and the territory reverted to Weimar. For close on seventy years, despite a population which had only grown to about 7,000 by the end of the century, Eisenach was the capital of an independent duchy in which the duke had absolute power. This power was strengthened by the town's comparative remoteness and the presence of a ducal militia ready to enforce their master's will. Roads were poor and travel difficult in the seventeenth century. Although the imperial post reached Eisenach in 1700, only the sick and women with children could travel by it, and all travellers were monitored. Indeed, the population at large was closely watched by the town council acting on behalf of the duke: anyone who stepped out of line was soon brought to order.

From 1672 Eisenach was therefore a *Residenzstadt* or royal seat, with its own royal household and government. In Bach's time there were four departments of state in Saxe-Eisenach: the privy council, the consistory (or church council), the rent office and the council for war, home affairs, taxation and mining. The household had its own department, with a marshal of nobility, ladies in waiting, pages and a corps of guards like any great court – and all this had to be paid for by the other unfortunate inhabitants out of their taxes.

A court also required musicians for church services, ceremonial occasions and royal entertainments, and Johann Sebastian Bach was born in Eisenach because his father happened to be employed as court trumpeter by the duke. Johann Ambrosius Bach was also a *Stadtpfeifer* or town musician in the employment of Eisenach council, hired to play on important municipal occasions such as the induction of new councillors, but his court employment was altogether more prestigious. It was also a good deal more restrictive. The year before Johann Sebastian's birth, his father had decided to return to the town of Erfurt whence he had come to Eisenach, but this required the duke's permission which His Highness would not give. So Ambrosius remained in Eisenach and his famous son was christened on 23 March 1685 in St George's Church.

Yet even if Ambrosius had not been ordered to remain where he was, it seems likely that Bach would still have been born in Thuringia like generations of his family before him. For musical Bachs had been colonizing the area since the end of the sixteenth century, when the first of the dynasty had sired a musical son named Johannes. Together with the nearby towns of Erfurt, Arnstadt, Schweinfurt and Ohrdruf, Eisenach was one of their main centres of activity.

The father of the first Johannes Bach – and the first of the clan to enter history, courtesy of his most celebrated descendant – was Veit Bach, a miller, said to have come from Hungary. We have this information from Johann Sebastian himself. In 1735 he composed an *Ursprung* or family tree of the Bachs which he transmitted to his son, Carl Philipp Emanuel. This tells us that Veit

> found his greatest pleasure in a little cittern which he took with him even into the mill and played while the grinding was going on. (How pretty they must have sounded together! However, it taught him to keep time, and that apparently is how music first came into our family.)

An extract from Bach's Ursprung *or Genealogy of his family, including the entry for his father (no. 11).*

The fact that Johann Sebastian troubled to make this record is significant, suggesting that he was proud of his descent and saw himself not in the romantic manner as a unique genius but as the inheritor of a family business. He was certainly proud of Veit's Magyar origins – and almost as certainly wrong about them. The name Bach was very common in Thuringia and it seems more likely that Veit had travelled to Hungary – perhaps in search of work or because of the political and religious strife which plagued Germany in the sixteenth century – and then returned to his native country where he settled in the village of Wechmar, which is about eight miles east of Eisenach.

Little more is known about Veit except that he died in 1619, having fathered Johannes Bach whose descendants were to proliferate throughout Germany for two and a half centuries and five generations – with such effect that, by the end of the seventeenth century, the name 'Bach' had come to be synonymous with 'musician' in Thuringia. The Bachs were not the only such dynasty in Germany, where music was a craft passed down from father to son (or even daughter) in the medieval fashion. The Ahles who dominated musical life in Mühlhausen, and the Lämmerhirts who hailed originally from Silesia, were comparable families, forgotten now except for their connections with Johann Sebastian. What distinguishes the Bachs is their extraordinary fertility and longevity, their higher than average output of first-class composers – and of course Johann Sebastian Bach himself. But however much Johann Sebastian may stand out even from his distinguished family, it is essential to bear in mind the idea of music as a craft with its own methods and mysteries if we are to understand his work and his attitude to it.

Bach family ties were strong. Not only were its members almost all professionally involved in musical life in one way or another; they helped each other to lucrative jobs and took in one another's children when disaster struck, as it often did in an age of high mortality. But this practical mutual help and family pride seem to have been grounded in a very real pleasure in each other's company. Johann Sebastian's first biographer Forkel describes how the members of the family would get together:

As it was impossible for them all to live in one place, they resolved to see each other at least once a year and fixed a certain day upon which they had all to appear at an appointed place. Even after the family had become much more numerous and first one and then another of the members had been obliged to settle outside Thuringia ... they continued their annual meetings, which generally took place at Erfurt, Eisenach or Arnstadt. Their amusements during the time of their meeting were entirely musical. As the company consisted wholly of cantors, organists, and town musicians who had all to do with the church, the first thing they did ... was to sing a chorale. From this pious commencement they proceeded to drolleries which often made a very great contrast with it. For now they sang popular songs, the contents of which were partly comic and partly naughty, all together and extempore, but in such a manner that the several parts thus extemporized made a kind of harmony together, the words, however, in every part being different. They called this ... a quodlibet, and not only laughed heartily at it themselves, but excited an equally hearty and irresistible laughter in everyone that heard them.

The ramifications of the Bach family are complex, confusing and mostly irrelevant to this story. All we need to know is that Johannes Bach, son of Veit, had three sons – Johann, Heinrich and Christoph – who established the dynasty in Erfurt and Arnstadt where they worked as town musicians and organists. Johann Bach married a member of the Lämmerhirt family, and Heinrich Bach was later singled out by Johann Sebastian's son, Carl Philipp Emanuel, as a lively character and a good composer. It was Christoph Bach, however, who was to be historically more significant as the father of Johann Ambrosius Bach and thus the grandfather of Johann Sebastian.

Johann Ambrosius Bach and his twin brother Johann Christoph were born in 1645. The portrait of Johann Ambrosius owned by his grandson, C. P. E. Bach, shows a determined and perhaps rather earthy man with the strong chin, thick neck, firm mouth and fleshy nose Johann Sebastian was to inherit from him. The view of the Wartburg which can be seen in the background of the painting emphasizes the sense of massive strength. A musician like almost all his many male cousins, Ambrosius was trained to play the violin by his father, and became town musician

A contemporary portrait of Bach's father,
Johann Ambrosius.

in Erfurt in 1667 while his twin brother took a similar post at Arnstadt. One year later Ambrosius married Maria Elisabeth Lämmerhirt, the daughter of a local furrier and town councillor. Although of straitened means herself, Elisabeth's cousins were men of substance and to that extent Johann Ambrosius had married well. In so doing he followed the example of his cousins, for the Bach dynasty was on a rising curve. The wife of the first Johannes had been an innkeeper's daughter but by the second half of the seventeenth century their descendants were establishing themselves as men of property and marrying into the middle classes. This instinct for acquisition Johann Sebastian was to inherit.

In 1669 Elisabeth and Ambrosius had their first child who died soon afterwards. Their second son, born in 1671 and named after his uncle Johann Christoph, was more fortunate. In the same year, Johann Ambrosius succeeded a cousin, Johann Christian Bach, as town musician in Eisenach – where yet another cousin, Johann Christoph, had already been organist at St George's Church for six years. According to the Eisenach town records, Ambrosius' duties were to play 'twice a day, at ten in the morning and at five in the evening, with his four men on the tower of the town hall, and to perform at church on all holidays and Sundays before and after the morning and afternoon sermons, according to the Cantor's instructions'.

Unable to afford a house of his own, Ambrosius took a cottage in Eisenach for his wife and son with rent paid by the town council. The house can still be seen at number 11 Rittergasse, a typical black-and-white three-storey cottage with a carved wooden frame on a sloping street. In a pattern which was to be repeated many times in Johann Sebastian's own life, the household was augmented by pupils and by other members of the two clans: Elisabeth's mother and Johann Ambrosius' mentally defective sister. In 1674 he bought a house of his own, facing the town brewery, and in consequence became eligible for citizenship as a *Burger* and taxpayer, with all the rights and obligations that status entailed.

The move is perhaps a sign not only of his own aspirations to property and social respectability but also of the esteem in which he was already held by his employers. When Ambrosius petitioned the duke of Saxe-

The 'Bachhaus' in Eisenach.

Eisenach, Johann Georg I, for permission to brew ale tax-free, his employers at the council recommended that permission be granted. The new town musician, they said, was not only 'conducting himself in a quiet and Christian way agreeable to everybody, but in addition he shows such outstanding qualifications in his profession that he can perform both *vocaliter* and *instrumentaliter* in church and in honourable gatherings in a manner we cannot remember ever to have witnessed in this place before'. This is high praise indeed from a body which seems to have ignored Ambrosius' cousin, the organist Johann Christoph. But Johann Christoph had lived a somewhat rackety and debt-ridden life, very unlike the steady Ambrosius. The council's admiration took practical form when, some months later, they suggested to the duke that during periods of royal mourning, when public performances of instrumental music were forbidden, Ambrosius should be compensated for loss of earnings.

The Bachs continued to have children at roughly two-year intervals until Johann Sebastian was born in 1685. He was the last of eight, only four of whom (three brothers and a sister) survived childhood. In addition, Ambrosius' duties required him to house and maintain two apprentices and two assistants. The deaths of his sister and his wife's mother eased pressure on the household. Nevertheless, they appear to have been replaced periodically by cousins, sent to stay at Eisenach in order to attend the school. This meant that there were often as many as fifteen people crammed into a small house. Despite the heavy expenses of his extended family, Ambrosius was eventually prosperous enough to employ a deputy to undertake certain of his minor duties, perhaps because he was so much in demand to perform at weddings, for which he was paid fees known as *Accidentien*. These fees were a vital part of most musicians' earnings, supplementing their regular but small emoluments from royal and municipal employers. They were to play an important role in Johann Sebastian's own career – both for better and for worse.

CHAPTER 2

Childhood and Education 1685–1702

L ike his own father before him – and as Johann Sebastian was to do in the fullness of time – Ambrosius Bach must certainly have taught his children the rudiments of music and instructed them in string-playing, but his youngest son's musical education was continued and refined by the boy's eldest brother. Johann Christoph Bach was a pupil of Johann Pachelbel, composer of the famous *Canon*. He became a distinguished organist, described in the church register at his death in 1721 as 'an artist of the first rank'.

Johann Sebastian's education was rigorous, both musically and academically. He was a highly intelligent, intellectually curious boy who responded well to the severe demands of the seventeenth-century curriculum. He progressed rapidly through school, and would have made a distinguished career at university had not family troubles and possibly his own inclination prevented matriculation. In 1692 he was enrolled in the Lateinschule – the grammar school – in Eisenach, which he attended together with his older brother Johann Jacob. Several members of the Bach family had preceded him there. It was normal for pupils to enrol at seven or eight, after progressing from a lower school, and to stay in each class until ready for promotion.

The Lateinschule was already a venerable foundation when Bach entered it, housed in a Dominican monastery from 1544 and celebrated throughout Thuringia. Despite such fame, facilities were by no means luxurious: huge classes were crammed into two small rooms where they sweltered in summer and froze in winter. School hours ran from 6.0–9.0 a.m. and 1.0–3.0 p.m. in summer and 7.0–10.0 a.m. and 1.0–3.0 p.m. in winter, with Wednesday and Saturday afternoons free. Sunday mornings were devoted to religious education and lengthy services in which the boys took part as choristers. Teaching was altogether more formal and more intensive than it is now. Much was learned by rote.

There was very strict discipline, though severe corporal punishment was relatively rare. Instead, a system of fines was firmly enforced: this proved to be an effective method of controlling poor boys who often had to earn not only their pocket money but anything more than bare subsistence.

The curriculum, extensively overhauled in the mid-seventeenth century, still looks comparatively medieval by our standards. Subjects included Greek, Latin and sometimes Hebrew, German grammar, logic, rhetoric, arithmetic and history. Each subject had its place in a carefully worked-out scheme, and within that scheme music played an important part. This was not to be the case for much longer. During Johann Sebastian's own lifetime, music moved from the centre of the curriculum to the periphery – a change which helps to explain some of the difficulties he experienced in his career as a choirmaster and teacher. The change in status is worth explaining, not least because Bach himself took the educational value of music – and its higher theory – very seriously indeed. His own works take account of both in a sublime combination of practical usefulness, unsurpassed beauty and technical sophistication.

In the Middle Ages the theory of music was at the very heart of the university curriculum, which was founded on the Seven Liberal Arts. These were divided into groups of three (the *trivium*) and four (the *quadrivium*) – seven, three and four being mystical numbers with special connotations in theology. The trivium comprised grammar, logic and rhetoric. These three disciplines were considered to be the foundations of eloquence, which was in turn the necessary preliminary to all other studies. This was not eloquence in the limited way we think of it now, as the power of persuasion. In ancient and medieval times, eloquence signified the far larger faculty of understanding and expressing ideas in language. The quadrivium included the four branches of mathematics: arithmetic, geometry, astronomy and music – four ways of articulating the essential harmony of the universe which was the primary object of knowledge. Between them, the subjects in the trivium and the quadrivium were thought to cover the entire domain of necessary learning outside theology (and its handmaiden, philosophy) to which they were subordinate. The purpose of medieval education was to bring the mind, and through it the soul, to knowledge of God. Within this framework music appears as an abstract science: the audible expression of geometrical relationships which are themselves the signs of a divine intelligence at work in the universe. Acquaintance with music is therefore a method of bringing the soul into communion with eternal wisdom.

It will be seen that this curriculum contains no science in the modern sense – physics, chemistry, geography; no practical subjects, and little of what we now think of as the liberal arts. It may also seem to be sternly theoretical, devoted to training students to master a body of arcane knowledge and to think and express themselves at the most rarefied level. Certainly, this is how the humanists of the Renaissance saw it, and their reforms of the education system were devoted to shifting the focus of the curriculum from theory to practice; from the contemplation of divine wisdom to the active life of man in the world. Music came to be seen less as a way of apprehending the divine order than as a vital means of worship – a change of emphasis which, in the longer term, inevitably promoted an interest in music for its own sake.

At the same time, the science of music began to disappear from formal university courses, though musical technique was still extensively taught in schools, especially in Germany. Even there, however, music was gradually being marginalized in a process which has culminated in our own approach to it as a pleasant optional extra in the school syllabus. In Bach's time, though advanced theory was largely restricted to specialists, there was still an acute awareness of the educational value of music, whether as a means of teaching or of worship, especially in the Lutheran Church and its scholastic foundations where the communal singing of the congregation was fundamental to the liturgy.

Furthermore, despite the shift away from a theological bias in education, schools and universities in the seventeenth century were still essentially religious institutions. Most were either attached to churches or, at the very least, profoundly influenced by their ecclesiastical origins. They were often required to provide music for those churches, a requirement which inevitably entailed extensive musical training for some if not all the boys. Music was therefore still an essential part of the syllabus; it was also a way of winning scholarships – and even a useful means of earning extra money.

At the Eisenach Lateinschule, as in all similar schools, there was a *Kurrende* or primary choir which sang simple tunes and one-part hymns, and a *chorus symphoniacus* which provided singers for the more sophisticated music used in full church services, mainly motets and cantatas. According to Forkel, who had the information from C. P. E. Bach, Johann Sebastian had an excellent soprano voice and soon graduated from the Eisenach Kurrende to the chorus symphoniacus, which meant that on Sundays he would find himself performing in St George's Church where his cousin Johann Christoph was organist and his father Ambrosius played violin or viola – reproducing in miniature, as it were, the Bach family's musical ascendancy and unity in Thuringia.

This unity was soon to be disrupted by death. In August 1693, one year after Johann Sebastian's registration at the Eisenach school, his father's twin brother died at Arnstadt. More painfully still, Johann Sebastian's mother Elisabeth died in May 1694. The consequent upheaval may be reflected in the school records which show many absences for the boy. Despite that, he was ahead of his elder brother in the class ranking. But there was further grief to come. Though Ambrosius was remarried within six months of his wife's death (to the widow of a cousin), he himself died in February 1695. Johann Sebastian was now an orphan.

Inevitably, this meant the splitting up of the Eisenach household. Ambrosius had prospered in his profession, but family illnesses and a daughter's wedding had involved him in heavy expenditure, and the council – once so ready to help – now declined to offer his widow any more than her legal entitlement: her late husband's salary for one and a half quarters. This was not enough to keep the household together even for a short time, and the new Frau Bach returned to the nearby town of Arnstadt whence she had come. Johann Jacob remained in Eisenach as apprentice to his father's successor, and Johann Sebastian went to live with his brother Johann Christoph, who was now organist at another nearby town.

* * *

Johann Sebastian remained in his brother's household at Ohrdruf for five years, attending an equivalent to the Eisenach grammar school. Ohrdruf resembled Eisenach in other respects. Part of an independent principality where the dukes of Saxe-Gotha and Altenburg reigned from 1640 to 1825, its social and political circumstances were similar in every way to a score of other Thuringian towns. The duke ruled as a benevolent despot through Johann Christoph's employer, the town council. Orthodox Lutheranism was the order of the day in church and state, there was a flourishing musical life in both and an excellent school – the Lyceum – where the two combined in a *chorus musicus*. This choir of the two dozen best singers performed on both private and civic occasions, earning substantial pocket money for its members – enough in Johann Sebastian's case to pay much of his way at home.

At the Lyceum in Ohrdruf the boy completed his education. Academic demands stimulated his high intelligence and capacity for hard work: though usually the youngest in his class, he was invariably placed among the highest-ranking students, rising rapidly through the school. When he became a senior pupil at 14, the average age of his classmates was 17.7 years. This precocity is noteworthy. Johann Sebastian had a mind which was both acute and profound, qualities which were later to characterize him as a composer. Naturally he did especially well in music lessons, despite the presence of a terrifying Cantor, Johann Heinrich Arnold, who punished the boys so severely that he was eventually dismissed for being what the school register uncompromisingly describes as 'a menace to the school, a scandal to the church, and a cancer in the community'. Arnold's successor was Elias Herda, a young man who had studied in the northern city of Lüneburg before returning to his home in Thuringia.

The young Bach also seems to have had a particular taste and talent for theology. On his death he was to leave a library in which the largest body of works was a collection of eighty theological treatises. Certainly, his critical intelligence fitted him for the kind of minute distinctions theology entails; and his compositions – especially the cantata settings – were later to reveal a delight in arcane theological matters. More importantly, music and theology went hand in hand from the start for

Bach. Both were ways in which God revealed Himself to the world and both were the province of rational enquiry. A belief in the universe as complex and often tragic, but essentially ordered and significant, is as fundamental to Bach's music as it was to his life. He might think of God's purpose as inscrutable but he could never conceive of it as irrational. In this sense, the order of his music reflects the order of the divine will.

Bach appears to have been a model pupil in every way. He was certainly no rebel. It is a modern assumption that artists are individualists, inevitably in conflict with authority and convention. Certainly, Bach had many squabbles in later life with employers and superiors, but these did not arise out of romantic hostility to authority as such. On the contrary, he accepted and supported the established order of which he was very much a part. He never seems to have doubted, for example, that he would become a musician and that successful musicians were rightly placed high in the social hierarchy. He quarrelled with others because he was a strong-willed and even stubborn man who insisted on his rights and argued for them in detail. No doubt his theological training proved useful in the nit-picking disputes he too often entered into.

In 1700, at the age of fifteen, Bach was withdrawn from the Ohrdruf school. According to the records he left for 'Luneburgum ob defectum hospitiorum' on 15 March. It seems that, despite Johann Sebastian's contributions to the housekeeping, Johann Christoph's growing household was simply too small to accommodate him. It is probably also true that Johann Sebastian was keen to set out in life; and, given the lack of funds, there was little chance of the university education which his father might have supported had he lived. It was therefore necessary to find a different route to the musical career which beckoned.

At this point the new Cantor, Elias Herda, came to the rescue. Good singers were always in demand for services at St Michael's Church in Lüneburg where Herda had studied. The church was attached to an academy for young noblemen and the *Mettenchor* (Matins choir) there provided a way of combining good music with good works, for it was stipulated in the statutes of the Ritteracademie that singers must be the 'offspring of poor people, with nothing to live on, but possessing good

The Michaeliskirche in Lüneburg as it was in Bach's time. Painting by J. Burmeister, c. 1700.

voices'. Choir members received free board and tuition, plus a small income which could be supplemented by the sort of *Accidentien* Bach had been earning in Ohrdruf. Herda recommended Johann Sebastian and another boy to the authorities at St Michael's and both were accepted as pupils. Although Lüneburg, just south of Hamburg, was 170 miles north of Ohrdruf – a huge distance in the seventeenth century – there was nothing unusual in this move. Thuringia was celebrated as a source of musicians, and singers and players were recruited from there to serve all over the empire.

Most of the journey was probably made on foot, but by April 1700, Johann Sebastian's name appears in the records of St Michael's Mettenchor. Lüneburg was an altogether grander and more sophisticated town than Ohrdruf or Eisenach. The church was a fine building with a

The Schloss at Celle where Bach performed in the court orchestra and became acquainted with French music. Drawing by G. Siebers, printed by A. H. Oetling, c.1830.

famous gilded altarpiece, the singing was of the highest standard, and there was an extensive music library established in 1555, which included scores by members of the Bach family. It is unlikely that the boy had direct access to this library – an inestimably precious possession in that age of scarce printed music – but it must have served to broaden the academy's repertoire and thereby introduced him to a far wider selection of styles and periods than he had yet known.

The students of the aristocratic academy conversed in French, adopted French manners and performed French plays and musical works. This Francophilia was encouraged by the ruling prince's liaison with a Frenchwoman. Georg Wilhelm of Lüneburg-Celle had a long-time French mistress, Eléonore Desmier d'Olbreuse, who carried the official title of the duke's 'friend' until he regularized the relationship by marriage. There is a connection with Handel here, because Georg Wilhelm's daughter, Sophia Dorothea, was to marry Handel's employer, the future George I of England. The duke and duchess lived some miles from Lüneburg, at Celle where they had striven to create the usual replica of Versailles. In addition, Eléonore had a grand town house in the city, where music was often performed. Herself a Huguenot, the duchess welcomed French refugees from religious persecution, and the theatre and orchestra at Celle were largely staffed by French artists.

Bach was probably taken to Celle by the confusingly named Thomas de la Selle, a pupil of Lully who taught dancing at the Ritteracademie and served as court musician at the ducal palace. He may also have heard French music in the duchess's Lüneburg house. What is certain is that he made his own copies of French organ works, including suites by Nicolas de Grigny and François Dieupart, at about this time. Such music – so very distinctive and quite different from the Thuringian style he was used to – broadened his horizons and contributed to the intriguing fusion of different manners which marks his own mature work.

These copies of French organ music are important for another reason. For it must have been during his time at Lüneburg that Bach began to develop into an organ virtuoso. His experience of performing at St Michael's was by no means confined to singing. Indeed, it was not long after his arrival that his voice broke and Johann Sebastian found himself more frequently employed as violinist and organist than as singer. Although he had already encountered the masterful organ-playing of his own cousin, Johann Christoph, it was while in Lüneburg that he met more widely celebrated and sophisticated players, including Böhm of the Johanniskirche, and Reincken of St Catharine's Church, Hamburg.

Georg Böhm was a fellow Thuringian, born in Ohrdruf and educated at the university of Jena where three of Bach's Ohrdruf teachers were his contemporaries. According to C. P. E. Bach, Böhm was greatly admired by Johann Sebastian, whose own early organ works show the older man's influence. Johann Adam Reincken was already seventy-seven when Bach walked the thirty miles to Hamburg to listen to him in 1701. This celebrated virtuoso's playing and improvisation made such an impression on the young man that he not only travelled from Lüneburg to Hamburg to hear Reincken several times while a student, but returned after his graduation to play for the elderly organist.

If Bach laid the foundations of a great performing career in these years, it was also at Lüneburg that he perfected his intimate knowledge of organ mechanism. During 1701 the instrument at St Michael's was overhauled by Johann Balthazar Held, a celebrated organ builder. Bach must have observed this work going on. Given his background, he had probably acquired considerable expertise before his arrival in Lüneburg, but an acquaintance with Held's work was an essential step in extending a mastery of mechanics and acoustics which was to reach legendary proportions in later years, when the mature Johann Sebastian was universally accepted as the leading German authority on organs in his day. Interesting in itself, this also reminds us that, for all the theoretical interests which were to loom so large in his work, Bach was a supremely practical musician who knew the instruments he wrote for quite literally from the inside. By the time he left Lüneburg he had little to learn about the fundamentals of instrumental construction and performing technique.

Engraving of an organist by Christoph Weigel, 1720.

What remained was to put this knowledge to good use in the professional world. By Easter 1702, Bach's studies at the Ritteracademie were concluded. The logical next step was the university course he had deferred earlier. Many years later, Johann Sebastian was extremely eager for his own sons to attend university, not least because he had not done so himself. Quite why he rejected further education, no one knows. Given his ability to finance himself, it seems likely that he had good reasons for deciding against a university course in favour of beginning work at once. There may have been family problems. Or possibly Bach was impatient to put his enormous gifts and his abounding energy to good use in the world instead of studying for several years more. He would not be the first talented boy to feel this way. However, his movements between the spring of 1702 and April the following year are unknown, so we can only speculate about motives. What is certain is that in 1703 he returned from Lüneburg to Thuringia. No doubt he was drawn there by tradition, nostalgia and family loyalty. The fact that there were also three vacant organ-lofts in the region, one of them at Eisenach, may have been another determining factor. Whatever the reasons for his return, he was now ready to begin his adult career in the land of his ancestors. He was just eighteen.

CHAPTER 3

The Apprentice 1702–8

The strength of Bach family influence in Thuringia made it almost inevitable that its talented new member would secure a post sooner rather than later. The only question was where. Whether he applied at Eisenach when his cousin Johann Christoph Bach died in March, we do not know; the job went to yet another member of the family. He did apply in July to the Jacobikirche in Sangerhausen, as we learn from a letter written many years afterwards. In this letter Bach reveals that the Sangerhausen council agreed to appoint him 'but that, in a move very characteristic of the relations between town councils and their masters, the duke of Saxe-Weissenfels intervened – after Bach had been promised the job – to secure the post for his own candidate. So Bach applied instead to the Neuekirche in Arnstadt where a new organ was nearing completion in 1703.

Bach's organ at Arnstadt.

While he was waiting for suitable work, Bach earned his living during the summer of 1703 as violinist in the court orchestra of Johann Ernst, younger brother to the duke of Weimar, doubling as a 'lackey' or servant when not required to play. This post, too, was probably secured through the complex network of family connections. Both Kapellmeister Drese and organist Effler at Weimar were friends, and at least one member of the orchestra was a distant cousin. In this respect the musical profession mirrored the complex network of relationships within the aristocratic world which employed it.

When the new organ at Arnstadt was ready, the mayor, Martin Feldhaus – yet another Bach kinsman – invited the eighteen-year-old Johann Sebastian to test it, as was the custom. In return for a fee and municipal hospitality, every new or restored organ was played and inspected by a distinguished expert who then wrote a report on the instrument which also constituted a certificate of worthiness. Bach was frequently in demand for this role in later years, and his reports were always lucid, detailed and precise. It is a tribute to his precocious reputation that he should have been asked to take on such a responsibility so early in life.

Though Bach had taken the opportunity to act as deputy to Effler at Weimar, the mayor was perhaps exaggerating when he described his young cousin in the receipt he drew up for Johann Sebastian's expenses as 'Princely Saxonian Court Organist' to the duke of Weimar. Such hyperbole was hardly necessary. Bach seems to have impressed his Arnstadt audience so deeply that the usual process of inviting several candidates to audition was bypassed and he was appointed organist of the Neuekirche on 9 August 1703. Five days later he began work.

His duties were comparatively light. He had to play the organ at morning services every Monday, Thursday and Sunday, and train the school choir for participation in the full choral service on Sundays. He also played in the band at the court of Anton Günther II. This left him plenty of time for composing, though comparatively little of Bach's surviving music dates from his time at Arnstadt. A number of chorale preludes belong to this period, as do the three *Partite diverse* for organ, though the clear influence of Böhm on these works suggests that they may have been composed even earlier. But the most interesting piece is the *Capriccio sopra la lontananza del suo fratello dilettissimo* ('Capriccio on the departure of a beloved brother', BWV992),* presumably written in 1704 on the occasion of Johann Jacob's departure from Eisenach to enter the service of Charles XII, king of Sweden, then campaigning with his army in Poland. This touching if naive keyboard work divides into a series of movements depicting the sadness of Johann Jacob's friends, their attempts to dissuade him from leaving, and the lively sound of his departure, echoed in the post-horn theme of the final fugue.

His yearly salary at Arnstadt was fixed at fifty florins, plus an allowance of thirty-four florins for board and lodging. This is more than his elder brother Johann Christoph ever earned at Ohrdruf and it suggests that Johann Sebastian had his eye firmly fixed on material advancement. Throughout his career he was almost always paid more than contemporaries in equivalent posts and he was always careful to enforce the smallest entitlement in his contract.

Arnstadt was a pleasant town, smaller than Eisenach, with a population of about 4,000, and blessed with fine buildings, and extensive gardens famous for their lime trees, fountains and grottos. The reigning prince was enlightened and his wife had close family connections with the cultured court at Celle. Attached to the castle were the usual museum and court orchestra and even that rarity, a small theatre, built by order of the princess. Bach also enjoyed a pleasant social life among his relations and their friends. Living in 'The Golden Crown' – the house of his cousin, the mayor – he encountered many members of the Bach clan.

On the other hand, his conditions of service soon proved to be most unsatisfactory. He worked in the poorest of the three churches in Arnstadt, with the weakest singers. Some of these singers were older than their nineteen-year-old master whose youth did not inspire them with respect, though an older man might have fared no better with the younger ones who liked to sneak out of church during the sermon to drink in a nearby tavern. This was not their only offence. An outraged town council minuted that the choristers

---

*The letters 'BWV' stand for *Bach-Werke-Verzeichnis* – Index to Bach's Works – and refer to the complete catalogue compiled by Wolfgang Schmieder.

have no respect for their masters, fight in their presence, behave in a scandalous manner, come to school wearing swords, play at ball games in their classrooms, even in the House of God, and resort to places of ill repute. Out of school they play games of hazard, drink, and do other things we shrink from naming.

Just like modern schoolboys, in fact.

These rowdies, led by a rude and unruly choir prefect who was supposed to keep them in order, were soon at loggerheads with the new organist, who resented them all the more because he was not, strictly speaking, obliged to train choristers, a task which fell to the Cantor. But the Arnstadt church had no Cantor at this time and the council seemed reluctant to appoint one, perhaps fearing the expense. The situation was not improved by Bach's volatile temper. As time was to show, Johann Sebastian could be an endlessly patient teacher at any level of ability where there was promise and application, but he did not suffer fools, slackers or third-raters at all gladly. Never an especially good disciplinarian, and reluctant to do more than the minimum, he was consistently but uselessly exhorted by his employers to try his best in what they admitted were unsatisfactory conditions.

The combination of Bach's laxity with mayhem among the choristers led eventually to complaints from the public about intolerable misbehaviour and poor musical standards. After two years of bickering between choristers, organist and town authorities about who was responsible for this state of affairs, things came to a violent head in August 1705 when Bach brought before the consistory court (the church council) his dispute with a chorister called Geyersbach, who also played the bassoon. It seems that there was already bad blood between the two when they encountered one another as Bach returned from performing at the castle one dark night. A hooligan three years older than Bach, Geyersbach had five other boys with him, and Bach was perhaps made more aggressive by the presence of his cousin Barbara Catharina who was walking with him. Fortified by beer and companions, Geyersbach chose this occasion to take exception to the choirmaster's disdainful verdict on his character and musical abilities as 'a nanny-goat bassoonist'. Insults were exchanged,

A view of Lübeck, the Baltic town where Bach visited Buxtehude.

the singer called the organist a dirty dog, attacking him with a stick, and Bach drew his sword. The two were pulled apart but Bach took his grievance to the consistory where the case dragged on for weeks. Meanwhile, he effectively gave up working with the choir, as he was strictly entitled to do. Eventually, he obtained permission from the town council for a month's leave of absence, and set off for the northern town of Lübeck in the autumn of 1705, leaving his cousin Johann Ernst to act as substitute organist. According to Forkel, Bach walked the 230 mile journey, but even for this young and vigorous man such a journey seems impossible in the time available.

The purpose of visiting Lübeck was to hear the Danish composer and organist Dietrich Buxtehude. Every year, on the five Sundays before and during Advent, Buxtehude directed a series of evening concerts – known as *Abendmusiken* – in his church, the Marienkirche. Founded in the mid-seventeenth century by Buxtehude's predecessor, Franz Tunder, and paid for by the merchants of Lübeck, one of the great trading cities of the Hanseatic League which dominated the commercial life of north Germany and the Baltic, these concerts featured large-scale choral and orchestral works with a magnificence which reflected the financial power of their sponsors. With forty instrumentalists at his disposal and a choir to match, Buxtehude provided Bach with musical experiences beyond anything he had yet known. It appears that the admiration was mutual, and that Bach might well have inherited more than a musical style, for Buxtehude hinted that the succession to St Mary's could be his, if only he would agree to marry the composer's daughter, Anna Margareta, then a woman of thirty. This sort of arrangement was common at the time, and Buxtehude himself had married Tunder's daughter on succeeding to the Marienkirche in 1668. But Anna Margareta had already been offered to Mattheson and to Mattheson's friend, Handel, without success. Bach, like them, declined her. Fortunately, Fräulein Buxtehude soon found a husband in the person of the splendidly named Herr Schieferdecker, who duly succeeded to the Marienkirche post and survived his wife to marry again.

Immersed in the musical life of northern Germany, Bach outstayed his leave by many weeks, returning to Arnstadt in late January 1706. Summoned in February to explain his prolonged absence to the authorities, he was also taxed with a new complaint, this time about his organ-playing. Evidently Bach had absorbed the lesson of Buxtehude's performances in Lübeck all too well, for instead of accompanying chorales simply he now varied the harmony and embarked on elaborate variations between verses and during services. Foreshadowing his later musical development, he also took to adding extra contrapuntal lines. When the church superintendent asked him to abandon these innovations which were confusing a congregation used to the

The title page of Buxtehude's Castrum Doloris, *first performed during Bach's visit to Lübeck.*

plainest music, Bach took offence and reduced his participation in the service to the barest minimum, for which he was again criticized. It seemed he could do no right.

Not surprisingly, he seems to have lost interest in his work at Arnstadt. Weary of continuing disputes with choir and council, and frustrated by the meagre musical resources at his disposal, he must have been unsettled by the brilliant grandeur of Lübeck which stirred his creative and professional ambitions and reminded him that there was a world beyond Arnstadt. It may also have been the case that he was not concentrating entirely on his work. One of his rows with the consistory involved a 'strange maiden' who was heard singing in the organ-loft – something absolutely forbidden in the days of all-male choirs. This maiden may well have been Maria Barbara Bach, an orphan born in 1684 who lived with her uncle, the mayor, in the house where Johann Sebastian boarded. Like Johann Sebastian, Maria Barbara was a great-grandchild of the first Johannes, so the two were second cousins, and she too had been raised in a musical household, her father being Johann Michael Bach, the church organist at Gehren near Arnstadt, and a more than competent composer.

It was Maria Barbara who helped Johann Sebastian out of his difficulties at Arnstadt, when an opportunity arose at the Blasiuskirche in the free imperial city of Mühlhausen following the organist's death in December 1706. Through her mother, Maria Barbara was related to a Mühlhausen councillor, Herr Bellstedt, who was prepared to recommend Johann Sebastian for the position. Invited to audition at Easter 1707, Bach was immediately successful. At the last minute he was almost prevented from taking up his post by a disastrous fire which destroyed 400 buildings – a large part of the city – and almost consumed the church. But the church was spared after all and on 15 June he was appointed organist at the Blasiuskirche. As the contract puts it:

> Now, seeing that the said Herr Bach has pledged himself by the shaking of hands to observe the conditions above written, we do hereby agree to pay him a yearly revenue of 85 gulden* in money, with the following allowances:

*A gulden is equivalent to a florin.

3 measures of corn
2 trusses of wood, one of beech, one of oak or aspen,
6 trusses of faggots, delivered at his door, in lieu of arable.

He was also provided with a wagon to move his belongings. Given his salary at Arnstadt, this was clearly a move upwards for Bach – not least because his distinguished predecessor had been paid only sixty-six gulden. Two weeks later he formally announced his new appointment to the Arnstadt council who accepted his resignation, which took effect in September. He was succeeded at Arnstadt by his cousin Johann Ernst who could only command half Johann Sebastian's salary.

Barely had the Mühlhausen cart carried Bach's few belongings from Arnstadt in early autumn, when another stroke of good fortune brought him an inheritance of fifty gulden from his uncle Tobias Lämmerhirt who died in August 1707. With this money and the prospect of his salary at Mühlhausen, Johann Sebastian and Maria Barbara were able to marry, which they did at a church in the village of Dornheim near Arnstadt on 17 October 1707. At the age of twenty-two, after what had turned out to be a false start, Johann Sebastian was ready to begin his career – and his life – in earnest.

* * *

At Mühlhausen Bach replaced the poorest, barest church of a provincial town with a magnificent city basilica, and he responded to his new situation by throwing himself into his labours. Finding only an antiquated collection of music in the church library, he devoted much time and energy to copying new pieces with the help of his pupil Johann Martin Schubart and his choir prefect. As at Arnstadt, the council had the rebuilding of the organ in hand, and this was the opportunity for Bach to write a remarkable report on its deficiencies which he presented to the councillors for their consideration. It is clear from this document how thorough and professional Bach's knowledge of organ construction already was. As Forkel puts it:

> He was very severe, but always just, in his trials of organs. As he was perfectly acquainted with the construction of the instrument, he could not

Bach's report on the organ of the Blasiuskirche in Mühlhausen.

be in any case deceived. The first thing he did in trying out an organ was to draw out all the stops and play with the full organ. He used to say in jest that he must know whether the instrument had good lungs.

Bach's intimate knowledge of the organ was certainly a factor in his extraordinary virtuosity, and of course in his compositional technique. For although we are inclined to think of him as a severely contrapuntal composer, concerned primarily with musical logic, all the evidence points to him being also a poet of sound, someone who liked to paint with the full palette at his disposal. The organ is an instrument of many colours and Bach was determined to exploit its capacity to the full. This is quite clear from one detail in the Mühlhausen report: his requirement that a carillon of twenty-six bells should be added to the pedal board. In a letter to Forkel, Bach's son Carl Philipp Emanuel observed that:

Organists were often startled at his idiosyncratic choice of stops when he wanted to try out their organs. They thought such a registration could not possibly sound well as he had planned it, but they soon heard an effect which astounded them.

The vital links between Bach's mastery of organ construction, his instrumental virtuosity, his compositional technique and his poetic sense, are made clear in the words which follow the passage just quoted from Forkel's biography:

66.
De Klokke-ftelder maakt met klinken
Een aangenaam geluyd voor 't oor;
Maar al dat lieffelijk rinkinken
Is met de lefte vinger door.

66.
Sonnes, beaux Carillons, fans ceffe,
C'eft un beau divertiffement;
Mais quand le Maiftre plus ne preffe,
A Dieu du Carillon charmant.

Cherub playing a carillon, from
Miroir des vertus et des arts,
a contemporary emblem book.

> After the examination [of the organ] was over, he generally amused himself and those present by showing his skill as a performer ... He would choose some subject and execute it in all the various forms of organ composition, never changing his theme, even though he might play without intermission, for two hours or more. First he used it for a prelude and a fugue, with the full organ. Then he showed his art of using the stops for a trio, a quartet, etc. Afterwards there followed a chorale, the melody of which was playfully surrounded in the most diversified manner by the original subject, in three or four parts. Finally, the conclusion was made by a fugue, with full organ, in which either another treatment of the first subject predominated, or one or two other subjects were mixed with it.

The organ music which has survived from this period reflects all the features mentioned by Forkel, ranging in scope from the strictest fugues to the freest improvisation.

Bach also composed a number of cantatas at Mühlhausen, including one for the installation of the new council in February 1708, *Gott ist mein König* (Cantata 71). The cantata was a standard vocal form at the time. Essentially dramatic in conception, each cantata tells a story and thereby illustrates a theme. Secular cantatas were usually written for soloist and the standard accompaniment of harpsichord and string bass (known as the *continuo*); but sacred cantatas were often more ambitious and varied, using orchestral accompaniments and setting complicated texts for a combination of choir and soloists. By Bach's time, the sacred cantata had become a fixture in the Sunday morning service of the Lutheran Church, and he was to compose hundreds of these works after taking up a post at Leipzig in 1723.

Cantata 71,* however, is a ceremonial secular cantata. Most unusually, the music was published, which perhaps suggests how seriously the councillors of this free imperial city took themselves. Their dignity requiring an unusually large orchestra, *Gott ist mein König* is a lengthy and elaborate homage to the new administration, based on a text from Psalm 74 which may have been assembled by Bach himself. The musical quality is uneven, as one might expect, but at least one of the choral numbers has frequently been singled out for praise as an example of Bach's taste and talent for illustrative music. 'Du wollest dem Feinde' seems to echo the cooing of the turtle-doves mentioned in the text, with delicate harmonies and sighing flutes and oboes. Otherwise, the cantata demonstrates the influence of Buxtehude, in particular that master's early immersion in Venetian music, as revealed by the sharp contrasts between different instrumental groups: two recorders and cello; brass; oboes and bassoon; and strings.

Gott ist mein König is not an especially distinguished work but in a different class altogether is Cantata 106, *Gottes Zeit ist die allerbeste Zeit* (BWV106), one of Bach's finest early pieces. It was probably written for the funeral of an old man and this has led some scholars to attribute it to the Arnstadt years on the grounds that it may commemorate Tobias Lämmerhirt, the uncle who left Bach a timely legacy in 1707. If so, it is a remarkably mature piece, a perfect elegiac ode lasting just twelve

---

*The numbering and dating of Bach's cantatas is still a contentious issue. Many have recently been assigned new dates by the scholar Alfred Durr, but they have yet to be renumbered. The numbers in this text refer to the BWV catalogue.

minutes. The sombreness of the subject is matched by the colouring of the orchestration which omits violins and violas in favour of the viola da gamba's deeper tones, and the score is full of marvellous pictorial touches. When the text speaks of the soul 'winging upwards', for example, the music climbs to the heights; when the singer proclaims her faith in eternal life, repeated notes emphasize her certainty.

If *Gottes Zeit* was performed for the burghers of Mühlhausen, however, it seems unlikely that they appreciated these musical subtleties – or approved of them if they did. For Mühlhausen was a city in which the religious battles of the previous century were still being fought, and music was one of the battlegrounds. The Treaty of Westphalia, in settling the conflict between Catholics and Protestants, had also freed both sides to pursue internal dissensions. In Mühlhausen these resulted in a bitter squabble between the two wings of the Lutheran Church, Pietist and orthodox. Like similar disputes throughout Europe, this turned – as the Pietists saw it – on the difference between simply believing in Christianity and actually living it, between intellectual assent and spiritual faith, between adherence to dogma and the personal conviction of salvation and damnation. Outwardly, these differences were expressed in the orthodox taste for full religious ritual, as compared with Pietist insistence on plain worship.

By the time Bach arrived in Mühlhausen, the Blasiuskirche was firmly in the hands of the Pietists, led by their pastor, Johann Adolf Frohne. But it seems likely that, although Bach got on well enough with Frohne, an unbigoted man who appears to have appreciated his new organist's talents, he himself inclined to orthodoxy. Certainly, the collection of theological books catalogued in his library after his death points in that direction, as does his friendship with Frohne's opponent, Archdeacon Georg Christian Eilmar, a leader of the orthodox party and the pastor of the Marienkirche. For many years before Bach arrived in Mühlhausen, Eilmar had been involved in a war of words with Frohne – a war of such ferocity that the council had been compelled to intervene. Yet this clerical hostility does not seem to have interfered with the friendship between the archdeacon and the composer. Even after Bach had left Mühlhausen,

Eilmar stood as godfather to one of his children, while Eilmar's daughter sponsored another. It is also possible that Eilmar assembled – or helped to assemble – the words for some of the Mühlhausen cantatas.

The situation was complicated for Bach by the fact that Pietists frowned on any but the most unpretentious music, as a distraction from worship and a sensual snare to the soul. They especially mistrusted chromatic harmony, instrumental accompaniment and melodic decoration, and would have confined church music at best to the simplest chorales, plainly accompanied. At St Blasius', under the long reign of Bach's predecessors, the Ahles, father and son, cantatas and voluntaries were simple in style. But – as the Arnstadt congregation had discovered – Bach favoured the more elaborate music he had encountered in Lüneburg, Lübeck and Hamburg, with decorated vocal lines, vivid instrumental colours and weighty choral passages, and he tried to introduce this sort of music at St Blasius', even though he and his pupil had to copy out the parts themselves. Frohne must have been appalled. Nor did it help in that era of intense local loyalties that Bach, unlike the Ahles, was not a native of Mühlhausen.

If Bach sided with the orthodox party because his theological tastes led him that way, and because orthodox Lutherans favoured music as part of God's justified tribute, we cannot doubt that the composer's enormous creative energy and intellectual curiosity were also significant forces determining his choice. How could these forces possibly be confined within the deeply felt but monotonous and often pallid music favoured by the Pietists? Bach was an ambitious man, constantly looking out for a post which would give him greater artistic scope, more money and higher social status – hence the move to Mühlhausen. But after less than a year in that city, he realized that he would have to move again. In the summer of 1708 an opportunity arose at Weimar where Johann Effler, the elderly *Hoforganist* with whom Bach had worked briefly in his first job, was retiring. A ducal court was socially more prestigious than most city churches and a court musician's salary likely to be higher than a church organist's. So Bach applied for the post in Weimar and, after the usual trial, he was appointed to the post in June 1708. After less than a year he was leaving Mühlhausen, taking his pupil Schubart with him and leaving yet another cousin in his place at the Blasiuskirche.

In the letter he wrote to the Mühlhausen city council – the 'Magnificence, High and Very Noble, High and Learned Sirs, High and Wise Sirs' whom he presumably addressed without irony – Bach requested permission to resign, observing in a famous phrase that he had

> always kept one end in view, namely, with all good will to conduct a well-regulated church music to the honour of God . . .

But this end had met with opposition which showed no sign of abating. He therefore thought it best for him to leave. Bach also made it plain in the letter that he considered his salary too small – which may have been a broad hint to the council that he might stay for more pay. If so, they did not take the hint, and one can only speculate on how musical history might have turned out had Bach remained a town organist. But perhaps the speculation is vain. A man of such energy and enterprise was not likely to confine himself to one job for a lifetime like so many of his contemporaries. And as if to underline the wisdom of his move to Weimar: when Bach took over Effler's duties he was paid almost twice the Mühlhausen salary, even though the old man remained titular court organist.

CHAPTER 4

The Court Composer, Weimar 1708–17

Although Bach was in an altogether more favourable situation at Weimar, his difficulties were not over. There were no religious quarrels in the duchy where the reigning duke, though theoretically in favour of toleration, enforced orthodox Lutheranism. But Wilhelm Ernst combined dogmatic orthodoxy with a Pietist fervour for the virtuous life in ways which could be tiresome for his subjects. He was by nature a solemn man, whose temperament had not been improved by his failure to produce an heir. Separated from his wife, he now lived alone. His

*Wilhelm Ernst of Saxe-Weimar
(1662–1728). Engraving, 1716.*

brother, for whom Bach worked briefly before taking up the Arnstadt post, had died in 1707 after a long illness (during which Wilhelm Ernst paid him not a single visit), leaving behind him two sons who lived with their mother in a small *Schloss* near the ducal castle. Ruling by divine right, the duke took his responsibilities very seriously indeed. Ducal decrees controlled every detail of existence for the citizens of Weimar who were liable to arrest and imprisonment for very minor infringements of the social and moral code, let alone the criminal law. Life at the palace was no less austere. Lights were extinguished at 8.0 p.m. in winter and 9.0 p.m. in summer, and there were few of the amusements traditional at court. On the contrary, gambling and philandering were severely punished. Wilhelm Ernst was especially careful to supervise the religious duties of his courtiers who were expected to attend daily service, taking turns to read lessons from the Bible. They learnt to pay close attention to the sermon about which they were likely to be questioned by their master, who even determined the order in which they took communion.

Eventually, this petty tyranny was to bring Bach and the duke into conflict, but to begin with the two men had an excellent working relationship. If the duke's regime was an unusually gloomy one, his very seriousness bore fruit in a genuine concern for the cultural life of his realm. His subjects gained little from this concern directly, though the duke did embark on schemes of improvement in the town for their welfare, including an orphanage, a college for teachers and a new grammar school. More characteristically, he replaced an old bearpit in the palace grounds with gardens which supplied him with fresh flowers every day. He also built up the library and the museum; and took a particular pleasure in music, both at court and in church. Frugal himself, he was prepared to spend on worthy social and cultural causes and, for the first years in Weimar at least, Bach was to benefit from this bounty.

Once again he began by extensively reconstructing an organ, this time in the palace chapel, though the instrument had only just been restored. It was first upgraded and then completely rebuilt to Bach's own specifications which, as usual, involved strengthening the colour, diversity and brilliance of the organ-stops. The rebuilding is symbolic of the way in which Bach the organist became absolutely his own man in the Weimar years, establishing a pre-eminent reputation as a performer, both in Weimar itself and far beyond. For the duke, however narrow his outlook in other matters, clearly recognized and appreciated Bach's extraordinary talent, and perhaps calculated that it could only reflect well on himself if publicized. Whatever the reasons, he allowed his organist frequent leave to

The Himmelsburg chapel at Weimar in Bach's time, since destroyed.

fulfil outside engagements playing and inspecting organs, on which occasions J. M. Schubart – the pupil Bach brought from Mühlhausen who was later to succeed him at Weimar – deputized for him at the palace. The duke also continued to increase his already substantial salary over the years – the surest sign that he wanted to keep Bach at Weimar.

Such was Bach's reputation as a virtuoso that by the time he left the city for Cöthen in 1717, stories of his diabolic powers were circulating throughout Germany. It was rumoured that when he played in village churches – as he frequently did – people would murmur: 'This can only be the devil or Bach himself.' Others left more substantial testimony to his powers – for example, the clergyman at Kassel who remarked that

> His feet flew over the pedal-board as though they had wings, and powerful sounds roared like thunder through the church. This filled Frederick, the Crown Prince, with such astonishment and admiration that he drew from

his finger a ring set with precious stones and gave it to Bach as soon as the sound had died away. If the skill of his feet alone earned him such a gift, what might the Prince have given him had he used his hands as well?

Bach's virtuosity on the pedals was well-known. Even one of his severest contemporary critics remarked on his extraordinary ability to perform the widest skips with both hands and feet without hitting wrong notes or contorting his body. According to Forkel,

> When asked how he had contrived to master the art to such a high degree, he generally answered: 'I was obliged to work hard; whoever is equally industrious will succeed just as well.'

This rather dour comment suggests that Bach, like other great performers, wearied of endless eager enquiries about the source of his virtuosity. He made a more dryly humorous answer to a similar question when he said:

> There is nothing to it. You only have to hit the right notes at the right time and the instrument plays itself.

His brilliance was recognized in many offers of employment. When he visited Halle in 1713, for example, his playing impressed the authorities so much that they not only offered him a job but even sent him the contract. Wilhelm Ernst prudently raised Bach's salary to 268 florins per annum and he declined the Halle post, though he visited the town again two years later to inspect a newly rebuilt organ. Such inspections were not merely a matter of prestige: they also brought in substantial fees and expenses. Bach might expect to receive sixty or seventy florins – a considerable sum when compared with his annual Weimar stipend, which was already generous. There was also an added inducement in the entertainment involved. The successful building or rebuilding of an organ was an occasion for civic celebration, and the inspectors were well wined and dined. Bach's second visit to Halle concluded with a magnificent banquet at which the three inspectors were served with:

Boeuf à la mode	Peas, potatoes, pumpkins,
Pike with anchovy butter sauce	asparagus, lettuce and radishes
Smoked ham	Fritters

Sausages and spinach	Candied lemon peel
Roast mutton	Preserved cherries
Roast veal	Fresh butter

There is every indication that Bach shared the hearty appetites of the period and enjoyed a good party.

These visits also provided him with the satisfaction of public recognition. This was all the more important because his activities as a composer – so much more significant for us today than his playing – remained in the shade. We can only wonder at this now, for it was in the Weimar years that he seems to have written many of his finest organ works. I say 'seems' because the dating of almost all Bach's works is still vexed, and none more so than the organ pieces. Many of the cantatas and the Passions at least have dates of first performance if not of composition. There are few such records for the organ pieces, and the order of their composition is the subject of much speculation based on stylistic evidence, the dating of paper, watermarks and so on. Unfortunately, stylistic evidence itself can be treacherous, because Bach was given to revising and even rewriting his keyboard works or adapting them from other media, and many exist in several versions.

The history of the organ works is further complicated by the fact that Bach was a brilliant improviser. The man who could improvise complex fugues for two hours at a time clearly had no need to write them down for himself. Only if they were for publication, for others to perform or for teaching, was a record necessary. Other pieces survive because they were copied out by pupils and admirers, or because Bach decided many years later to organize them in collections, at which point they were often revised. We have to assume, therefore, that the organ works we actually have represent only a proportion, albeit a substantial one, of the music Bach composed: others were either lost or never written down.

Nevertheless, scholars are agreed that the bulk of Bach's greatest organ works were written or begun during the Weimar years, including such popular masterpieces as the 'Dorian' Toccata and Fugue in D minor (BWV538), the Toccata and Fugue in F major (BWV540), the Fantasia and Fugue in G minor (BWV542), the wonderful Passacaglia in C minor

*Arcangelo Corelli (1653–1713)
whose music influenced both Bach
and Handel. Portrait attributed
to Hugh Howard.*

(BWV582) and the Prelude and Fugue in C major (BWV545). Many individual chorale preludes also date from the Weimar years, and the collection of similar pieces which make up the *Orgel-Büchlein* (BWV599–644) was begun at Weimar and concluded (though never completed) later.

At Arnstadt and Mühlhausen Bach had been discouraged from performing sophisticated music during church services, but there was no such prohibition at Weimar where the duke relished church ceremonial as befitting God's glory and his own taste for dignified worship. The conditions were therefore ripe for a flowering of Bach's interest in the chorale prelude, a form which allowed him to combine his lifelong concerns with contrapuntal forms, the musical expression of ideas, and theology.

The chorale preludes, which Bach composed and revised throughout his life, also provided a forum for experiment and innovation. The form evolved from the practice of introducing the congregational singing of the chorale – the hymn central to the Lutheran rite – with an instrumental preamble. In the late seventeenth century, these preambles became more and more elaborate; organists also acquired the habit of playing interludes between the verses and decorating the tune with descants. The result was the emergence of an instrumental genre in which the chorale tune serves as a base or *cantus firmus* for more or less complex musical development. Bach's chorale preludes range from the simplest harmonization of a tune, to the most intricate contrapuntal textures. He often used the same tune for several different pieces. *Vom Himmel hoch, da komm' ich her*, for example, occurs in various incarnations, culminating in the remarkable Canonic Variations written during the last years of his life.

As time passed, Bach became increasingly preoccupied with the idea of deriving the music of the chorale preludes from the words of the tunes on which they are based. They cease to be mere decoration or elaboration of the hymn-tune and become commentary on it. As one of his Weimar pupils, Johann Gotthilf Ziegler, afterwards organist at Halle, remarked in 1746: 'Herr Kapellmeister Bach, who is still living, instructed me when playing hymns not to treat the melody as if it alone were important, but to interpret the words through the melody.' Sense and sound were as one.

It was also at this time that the composer started to develop that blend of diverse styles which eventually produced the masterpieces of his mature years. The chorale prelude is a distinctively *German* form. Since his years at Lüneburg, however, he had also been studying the equally distinctive school of *French* organ music, transcribing works by de Grigny and Dieupart. The latter's influence can be seen in the prelude to the first English Suite, which is based on the gigue from Dieupart's first *Suitte de Clavecin*.

Antonio Vivaldi (1678–1741) sketched by P. L. Ghezzi, 1723.

However, the single most important aspect of his musical development at Weimar came from a study of *Italian* music, and Bach's mature work – especially his organ music – represents what is perhaps a unique fusion of these three very different traditions. From composers such as Legrenzi, Corelli, Bonporti, Albinoni and Frescobaldi, he took themes for organ improvisations. He also imitated and experimented with Italian styles and genres, as in the Pastorale in F major (BWV590), which recalls the gentle mood and siciliano rhythm of Corelli's *concerti grossi*.

The title page to J. G. Walther's Musikalisches Lexicon, *1732.*

Bach had encountered these different types of music before, of course – both directly in Lüneburg and elsewhere, and indirectly through their influence on the work of his own teachers – but his specific discovery in Weimar was the Italian concerto for soloist and ensemble. These concertos were appearing in huge numbers during the first three decades of the eighteenth century, and Bach and his Weimar friend Johann Gottfried Walther studied them together. A distant relation of Bach's through the Lämmerhirts, Walther was organist at the Stadtkirche and a fine composer. He was also compiler of the *Musicalisches Lexicon*, one of the first musical dictionaries, which contains the earliest biographical notice of Bach himself. Bach stood as godfather to Walther's son and the two men shared their musical experiences. Before leaving Weimar, Bach presented his friend with more than 200 compositions by Böhm, Buxtehude and others, many of them copied out in his own hand.

According to Walther, the two men engaged in friendly rivalry over arrangements of violin concertos for keyboard. Among surviving examples of Bach's arrangements are works by Vivaldi and the Marcello brothers, and by Bach's young pupil, Prince Johann Ernst of Weimar. But 'arrangements' is perhaps the wrong word. For Bach, arrangement meant far more than simple transcription of notes from one instrumental medium to another. The transfer from violin to keyboard involved a complete rethinking in terms of his own style. Italian music was essentially melodic, comparatively simple harmonically and eschewing complex counterpoint in favour of flowing lines and occasional dramatic gestures. Bach enriches the harmonic texture of his models, adds melodic and contrapuntal details, and virtually recomposes some of the movements.

His encounter with Vivaldi was later to bear fruit in the Brandenburg Concertos and other orchestral works, and it reminds us that the organ was not the only object of his interest at Weimar, where the court gave him wider opportunities to experiment with vocal and instrumental music. At first he was involved only as a performer. His main appointment was as Hoforganist; but, according to contemporary documents, he also served as chamber musician, a post which involved playing in the ducal band of sixteen musicians who were required to dress in Hungarian hussar uniforms for their appearances. Their director was the Kapellmeister, Johann Samuel Drese, an elderly man whose son served as his deputy. Johann Sebastian, however, had been raised to the intermediate rank of *Konzertmeister* when he turned down the Halle offer, at which time he began to share with young Drese the duty of composing new works for the court. Drese provided secular music while Bach was expected to produce a new cantata each month for performance in chapel. For these performances, the dozen-odd members of the ducal choir were joined by the band, providing Bach with extensive experience in composing for and conducting mixed forces. Only about twenty or so Weimar cantatas survive, half solo works and half with chorus. Perhaps the most interesting is Cantata 21, *Ich hatte viel Bekümmernis*, composed for the visit to Halle. This is remarkable not only for its beauty but because, most unusually, it seems to show the direct influence of a work by Bach's great contemporary, Handel, whose opera *Almira*, performed at Hamburg in 1705 and 1713, had enjoyed an enormous success in Germany. We do not know whether the reference to *Almira* is accidental or deliberate; but we do know that Zachow, the man Bach was invited to succeed at Halle, was Handel's teacher, so the music may well be a graceful and very characteristic tribute to him.

A portrait of Bach c. 1715, attributed to J. E. Rensch the elder.

Silhouettes of Johann Sebastian and Maria Barbara Bach by an anonymous artist.

Bach's personal and social life during his years at Weimar was comfortable, interesting and fulfilled. Weimar was a very handsome city – it still is – and not a very large one: with a population of about 5,000 it was then smaller than satellite towns such as Eisenach. But as a centre of government and the seat of an important reigning prince, it was altogether more metropolitan in aspect than any of Bach's earlier places of residence, even the city of Mühlhausen.

Domestically, Johann Sebastian and Maria Barbara settled down to ample family life. They had six children at Weimar, including twins who died almost immediately and two boys who were to become celebrated as composers: Wilhelm Friedemann (1710–84) and Carl Philipp Emanuel (1714–88). Each in his own time was to be more famous than his father, though both have since retreated into Johann Sebastian's shadow. There is reason to believe that this shadow was a dark one. Not that Bach was anything but a devoted, kind and loving father, but he was also a very strong character with decided views, and paramount in his own profession. All these factors made life difficult for his children, especially for sons following in their father's footsteps. By the mid-eighteenth century the notion of music as a craft was already giving way to more romantic ideas of self-expression, which invariably suggest reaction against the established order. For Bach's sons their father must have represented the established order in every sense, paternal and musical.

The normal father–son tensions – which Bach himself had escaped by reason of his own father's early death – were thus likely to be exacerbated for boys destined for the same profession. At least two seem to have suffered accordingly. To judge from his enthusiastic discussions with Johann Sebastian's first biographer Forkel, Carl Philipp Emanuel came to terms with his father's legacy and made a life and career of his own. Despite considerable success as a composer, Wilhelm Friedemann did not. An unhappy man, he was to lead an unsettled existence, though not quite so disastrously as the last of Bach's children born in Weimar. Johann Gottfried Bernhard (1715–39) was yet another musical Bach, but one who was to bring disgrace on the family name and escape serious trouble only by dying young.

At Weimar, all these problems were in the future. Except for the death of infants, a commonplace event in the eighteenth century, Bach's family life was happy and secure. C. P. E. Bach told Forkel that the house was 'like a beehive and just as full of life'. Besides the immediate family, the house contained two young cousins, including Bach's nephew Johann Bernhard, the son of his own teacher and elder brother, Johann Christoph. This boy was being trained to the profession by his kinsman, just as Bach himself had been. Johann Bernhard became a favourite pupil of Bach's and in time succeeded his father as organist at Ohrdruf. One of Maria Barbara's sisters eventually joined the household and other pupils came and went, including two who were to succeed Bach at Weimar.

It was during his years at Weimar that Bach became celebrated as a teacher – so much so that one cantor walked to the town from a local village to take lessons twice a week for seven years. Bach taught keyboard and composition, and to both he brought his incisive mind, endless energy and passion for detail. Keyboard pupils had to begin by learning how to hold their hands over the keys with the three middle fingers curved inwards. They were encouraged to keep their hands rounded and to move them as little as possible, so as to develop the responsiveness, strength and flexibility of the fingers. Based on organ technique, this method proved a sound basis for playing both harpsichord and clavichord. Showy playing was firmly discouraged. Lessons began with finger exercises and then with little pieces which Bach wrote to develop particular skills. These preliminaries might continue for months until the pupil had reached a satisfactory level of achievement. More complicated pieces which Bach called 'Inventions' would then be introduced, the teacher often playing them over himself to show how they should sound. Finally, pupils were allowed to start on Bach's own keyboard masterpieces, the French and English Suites, the Partitas, the *Well-tempered Clavier*. One pupil recalled Bach playing this last work to him no fewer than three times. But, as he remarked, so beautiful was the playing that the hours seemed to pass like minutes.

About Bach's method of teaching composition we have several testimonies, including his own, which he recorded at the end of the *Clavierbüchlein* he wrote for his second wife Anna Magdalena, and remarks Carl Philipp Emanuel made to Forkel. As with his clavier teaching, the keys to his approach were method and application. Pupils began by writing four-part harmony on the model of Bach's own chorales. They would be given one or more of the parts – soprano, alto, tenor and bass – and asked to supply the rest. Each part was written on a separate line or stave to show up its melodic shape, because Bach would not tolerate dull part-writing: without transgressing the rules, each voice had to have a proper line of its own. He reminded his pupils that every part was like a speaking voice which must shape its sentences grammatically and say nothing unless it had something to say. Until the techniques of four-part harmony and basic counterpoint were mastered, students were not allowed to compose music of their own. When they did so, they were told not to begin writing down the notes until the piece had been thought through. Improvising at the keyboard as a means of composition was discouraged, and Bach especially despised what he called 'Clavier Horsemen' who let their fingers wander over the keys in search of ideas.

The connection between performance, composition and tuition is vividly illustrated by the case of the *Orgel-Büchlein* ('Little Organ Book'), assembled between 1713 and 1716, and so called not because it was written for a little organ or because the pieces are short, but because the manuscript notebook in which Bach wrote the pieces was a small one.

Bach's MS transcription of Vivaldi's Concerto grosso in D minor, op. 3, no. 11.

Just as Brahms was inclined to speak of his massive symphonies and concertos as 'little' pieces, this may well be a joke on Bach's part. This work was originally meant to include 164 chorales covering the whole of the liturgical year, and Bach began by writing their names in order on successive pages, allowing a single page for each. The work was begun in Weimar but discontinued at Cöthen after only forty-five chorales had been composed. Written in Bach's own hand, the title page reads:

LITTLE ORGAN BOOK

wherein an organ student is instructed how to develop in sundry ways a chorale and, at the same time, gain experience in use of the pedals, which in each of these chorales is treated as entirely obbligato.

The six English Suites were also written at Weimar. It is even conceivable that Bach had the idea of publishing the collection of suites as a set when he began to compose them. This was common practice at the time, and in later life he began to organize much of his work in collections for the purpose.

As his pupils were to testify, Bach clearly enjoyed his strenuous work. In the little time he had to spare from playing, teaching and composing, his social life in Weimar was also congenial. Though strictly governed, the town was a civilized place to live, at least for the privileged classes, and there were enough distinguished men in Weimar to provide Bach with intellectual stimulation – something he relished, as his library shows.

Chief among these was Salomo Franck, secretary to the consistory, ducal librarian and curator of the palace collection of coins, medals and curios. Franck was a poet, the author of many hymns and – crucially – of two volumes of cantata libretti. Bach used one of them for his Easter Day Cantata (no. 31) in 1715, and continued to draw on them throughout his time at Weimar. Franck's texts are quite different from Eilmar's. Mystical, full of deep feeling and references to nature, they are closer to Pietism than to orthodoxy, which suggests that Bach, though orthodox, was by no means dogmatic. It is also the case that, like other composers before and since, he was looking for the best words for setting to music, not the most ideologically correct. Franck's libretti provided strong dramatic structures and opportunities for the kind of word-painting Bach enjoyed.

Other friends in Weimar included J. C. Kiesewetter, formerly Bach's teacher at Ohrdruf and now Rector of the new Weimar grammar school; and Johann Matthias Gesner, an admirer of Bach's music who also taught at the school. The time for social life was limited, however, for Bach was also composing prolifically. Many works have been lost from these years, either through misfortune or because they were not deemed valuable enough to be worth preserving. Others later disappeared from the keeping of Wilhelm Friedemann, who inherited a large share of his father's manuscripts after Johann Sebastian's death. Among works which have survived are the Brandenburg Concertos, which Bach began composing in about 1713, completing the set after his move to Cöthen.

But despite all these advantages – his growing reputation, opportunities to perform and compose, happy family life, secure and substantial income – all was not well with Bach in Weimar. However much his ducal patron admired and sympathized with the Konzertmeister, he was also a tyrant who expected the absolute submission which a man of Bach's character was not inclined to give. Bach was no rebel. He could be diplomatic and even submissive when he wanted to. The elaborate language of some of his letters to officialdom – which can strike us now as grovelling – shows that he knew what line to take when necessary. But he also insisted absolutely on the letter of his rights and – just as much as the duke himself – demanded the proper respect due to him. If Wilhelm was appointed to his station in life by God, then so was Johann Sebastian Bach. And where his work and his status were concerned he could be immovably stubborn. He also seems to have been somewhat contrary, in the sense that he met challenges head on when there was no chance of victory. So it was almost inevitable that, as the years passed, his relations with Wilhelm Ernst, once so cordial, would deteriorate.

Ernst August of Saxe-Weimar.
Engraving by J. C. Sysang, 1742.

Ironically, the chief cause of grievance between them sprung from Bach's friendly relations with the household of Ernst August, the duke's heir. Uncle and nephew were on the worst of terms. The founding charter of the Weimar duchy in 1629 had vested power in the duke, at the same time giving the male members of his family a consultative role in government. This was designed to unite the dynasty, but was also a formula for trouble when relationships were bad – which in Weimar was almost invariably the case. Since by law the head of the family retained absolute power, the consultative role of the others was productive of little save irritation on both sides. Sometimes the problem could be solved by giving cadet branches estates of their own, as at Eisenach. Otherwise friction was unavoidable.

So it was that Wilhelm Ernst had ruled with the 'advice' of his younger brother Johann Ernst, known as the *Mitregent*, until the latter's death in 1707, when the co-regency passed to his eldest son, Ernst August, then a minor. Ernst August and his brother were both musical and both took lessons from Walther and Bach. But Johann Ernst the younger died in 1715, aged only nineteen. This was a real loss for Bach, personal and musical, as the boy was a fine performer and composer – so fine that, for many years, several of his violin concertos, transcribed for keyboard by Bach, were mistaken for compositions by Vivaldi. Ernst August survived long enough to inherit the dukedom from his uncle – and this was at the root of the bitter trouble between them. For, as is often the way, ruler and heir got on very badly indeed and the young co-regent exercised his right to criticize the reigning duke's policies at every opportunity. This made life difficult for courtiers. With one eye on their present master and another on the future, they tried to please each prince without antagonizing the other, a balancing act complicated by the fact that some government functions in Weimar were financed from a treasury controlled jointly by uncle and nephew.

Perhaps unsurprisingly, the two men were somewhat similar characters. Like his uncle, Ernst August was autocratic, often arbitrary and sometimes downright bizarre. He believed firmly in a monarch's right to rule absolutely and when he succeeded Wilhelm Ernst he issued an edict prescribing six months' imprisonment for any subject foolish enough to complain about conditions in Weimar. Nevertheless, he was on good terms with Bach, as was his wife who stood as godmother to Johann Sebastian's son Leopold Augustus. This was an honour for Bach but not a wise move. Wilhelm Ernst, engaged in a running battle with his nephew which by this time extended to petitioning the emperor and arresting one another's officials, had forbidden the courtiers to have any intercourse with the rival court at Ernst August's castle, the Rotes Schloss. Musicians were banned from playing there, on pain of a ten thaler fine – unfair in itself, given that they were paid from the joint treasury. But Bach simply ignored the order. And as if to underline his defiance, on Ernst August's birthday he bypassed the court entirely, performing a cantata at the Rotes Schloss with musicians invited from nearby Weissenfels. To add insult to injury, at the end of this ceremony he presented the heir with a poem bound in green taffeta. The ducal castles were only a few hundred yards apart. There could not have been a clearer snub to Wilhelm Ernst, who did not pretend to ignore it.

Such open defiance was bound to infuriate the irritable duke, who took his revenge in December 1716 when old Drese, the Kapellmeister, died. Bach must have expected to succeed Drese. Not only had he been appointed effective number two, as Konzertmeister. He was far and away the most distinguished musician in Weimar and recognized as such throughout Germany. He certainly far outshone both the Dreses, as he had once outshone the Ahles. The duke, however, decided otherwise, and Bach could hardly have been surprised in view of his defiant behaviour. First, Wilhelm Ernst tried to secure Telemann for the post. When that master declined it, he gave up the search and appointed young Drese. In the context of a system which gave preference to heredity, Drese certainly had a claim on the post by right of blood. But Bach's claim by right of talent was much stronger, and the duke's application to Telemann showed that he was prepared to ignore traditional father–son succession to get a first-rate Kapellmeister. It also showed that the time had come for Bach to move on. But where to? Where else could he find such excellent terms of employment? Perversely, the answer to this question lay – like many of his problems – in the ducal house itself.

CHAPTER 5

The Court Composer, Cöthen 1717–23

Several times during his years at Weimar, Bach was required to accompany Wilhelm Ernst on royal visits. In 1714 the court journeyed to Kassel, and in January 1716 to Nienburg, a small town on the banks of the river Saale, for the marriage of the duke's heir, Ernst August, to a widowed sister of young Prince Leopold of Anhalt-Cöthen. The Weimar musicians travelled with the court and performed for the wedding at which Prince Leopold was present. In the following month they also accompanied Wilhelm Ernst on a visit to Saxe-Weissenfels, where Bach's delightful cantata *Was mir behagt* (BWV208) was performed for the birthday celebrations of the reigning duke. Once again, Leopold and his sister were in attendance and it is clear they were both deeply impressed by Bach and his music – so impressed that the impetuous Prince Leopold determined to offer Bach a senior post at his court.

Listening to *Was mir behagt* today, one can still hear what pleased

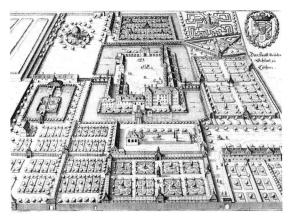

Das fürstl Resider Schloß zu Cöthen

The palace and garden at Cöthen where Bach worked for six years, engraved by M. Merian.

Prince Leopold. The words by Salomo Franck are by no means inspired, the text consisting largely of the judicious flattery princes expected and got in those days. But the music is superb, and Bach himself clearly valued the work which he used in various forms on other occasions. In the same year as the Saxe-Weissenfels visit, for example, it was performed again at the birthday celebrations for Duke Ernst August. Twenty-five years later, the composer was still bringing it out for royal occasions such as a visit to Leipzig by the elector of Saxony in 1742. He also plundered the music for at least four other works, including a religious cantata (no. 68) and a piece for violin, oboe and continuo (BWV1040). Although the whole of *Was mir behagt* is not often performed today, many people are familiar with the work in the form of arrangements from one especially charming aria, 'Schafe können sicher weiden' (Sheep may safely graze).

The prince had succeeded his father at Cöthen in 1704 as a child of ten, but until December 1715, when Leopold came of age, his mother acted as regent of the tiny state which was carved out of the duchy of Anhalt in 1603. Following her late husband's example, Princess Gisela Agnes ruled frugally; given an annual income of 7,600 thalers, she could do little else. The princess lived as befitted a pious widow, concentrating on religious duties and good works. Cöthen was a small but handsome place, with the royal residence situated in the centre of the town but separated from it by a moat. The princess saw that the people were well cared for, establishing a school and a home for impoverished gentlewomen. There was no theatre, opera or orchestra at the court, but her one concession to a son besotted with music from boyhood was to appoint three musicians to her establishment in 1707.

Because Cöthen, situated about eighty miles north-east of Weimar, came within the king of Prussia's sphere of influence, in 1708 Leopold was sent away to be educated in Berlin where he attended the Ritter-academie, a school for Prussian noblemen. His education concluded with the Grand Tour which was usual for European aristocrats at this time, taking in England, France, the Low Countries and Italy on a journey which was meant to be both pleasurable and instructive. While travelling, Prince Leopold polished his skills as a performer on violin, bass viol and harpsichord, and in Rome took composition lessons from the German composer Heinichen, a former pupil at the Leipzig Thomasschule.

Returning to Cöthen in 1713, the eighteen-year-old Leopold set about reviving court life. Eager to make a show in the world after the austerities of his mother's regime, and loftily indifferent to the small size of his revenues, he enlarged the library and the art collection with items brought back from his tour, and commissioned agents to buy others. But music was his ruling passion, his ambition to make Cöthen a great musical centre. He began by supplementing his mother's modest ensemble with a band of first-rate players, including several from Berlin where the new king of Prussia, disliking music as fiercely as Leopold loved it, had recently disbanded his court orchestra. In July 1714 Leopold created the post of Cöthen Kapellmeister for Augustin Reinhard Stricker, also from Berlin, at the same time appointing Frau Stricker court soprano and lutanist.

By 1716 the Cöthen *Kapelle* numbered eighteen players. In August the following year the Strickers retired, and the way was thus open for Leopold to offer Bach the post of Kapellmeister. The terms were highly favourable: 400 thalers per annum, as opposed to less than 300 thalers at Weimar – and it is worth remembering that the Weimar remuneration was already four times what he had been paid at Mühlhausen. Bach's Cöthen salary equalled that of the second highest official, the court

Bach as Cöthen Kapellmeister, painted c. 1720 by J. J. Ihle.

marshal. It not only exceeded the combined wages of Herr and Frau Stricker by 120 thalers per annum but represented five per cent of what had been Princess Gisela's entire revenue! Bach was also a figure of social consequence. A Kapellmeister ranked comparatively high in the pecking order in a tiny state like Anhalt-Cöthen, especially if he were a personal friend of the prince. When Bach's seventh child was christened, the godparents included three members of Leopold's family, a court councillor and a court minister – all members of the aristocracy.

There was the added bonus that Bach escaped from royal squabbling at Weimar and the oppressive rule of Wilhelm Ernst. He was also free of religious tyranny. Calvinism was the established religion at Cöthen, but Leopold was the child of a mixed marriage, the dowager princess being a Lutheran who had lobbied during her husband's lifetime for the rights of co-religionists. Her activities, notably the establishment of a Lutheran school, caused friction between the two communities and antagonized the Calvinist church consistory which governed religious matters in Cöthen. There were rows about the distribution of church taxes and the use of bells. None of this, however, affected Bach. As the child of parents who had agreed to disagree, Leopold took a comparatively liberal view of religious observance, which meant in practice that he rose above the angry arguments of his people. He believed, as he said, that the greatest happiness of his subjects depended on their freedom of conscience being safeguarded. But even if the prince had not taken this view, there would have been little call for Bach's involvement in the official church: Calvinist services took place in undecorated chapels and employed the bare minimum of music: no voluntaries, no anthems or cantatas, only the occasional plainly accompanied hymn.

Bach's duties at Cöthen therefore focused almost entirely on secular music. His task was to conduct the princely orchestra, supplemented with a small choir when necessary, and to provide music for regular concerts and entertainments and for special occasions, such as the prince's birthday. Furthermore, whereas he had previously composed much organ and vocal music, he was now to devote himself mainly to instrumental works, ranging from solo sonatas to concertos. He continued to play the organ and to inspect instruments, but his career as a full-time organist was over, never to be resumed. With apt symbolism, the organ in Prince Leopold's palace chapel was an insignificant instrument by Bach's standards, and no attempt was made to upgrade it, as had been done at Arnstadt, Mühlhausen and Weimar. The change was momentous for a man who had spent his first thirty-two years exclusively within the musical orbit of the Lutheran Church.

Bach was appointed Kapellmeister on 5 August 1717, but before he could take up the post, two things happened. The first confirmed his pre-eminence, the second dispelled any doubts he might have had about leaving the comparatively cosmopolitan city of Weimar for the tiny state of Cöthen. Early in the same year, the French organist Louis Marchand was dismissed from royal service at Versailles. Apparently an arrogant, bad-tempered, loose-living man, Marchand had neglected his wife so scandalously that the French Regent, the duc d'Orléans, assigned her half the organist's salary, upon which Marchand had reportedly closed the organ in the middle of a service at Versailles, remarking: 'If my wife receives half my stipend, let her play half the service.' Banished from the court for impertinence, he turned up later in Dresden, the capital city of Saxony, about ninety miles east of Weimar.

It is not known whether it was by design or chance that Bach visited Dresden at the same time as Marchand, a few weeks after his appointment at Cöthen. What is certain, according to Bach's own testimony, is that he challenged Marchand to a duel at the keyboard, offering to play at sight any music put before him if Marchand would agree to do the same. The Frenchman accepted the challenge and a public concert was duly arranged in the house of a local aristocrat. Such competitive trials of skill were not uncommon at a time when instrumental virtuosity was rapidly increasing and public concerts were becoming popular. But the contest was not to take place. On the morning of the appointed day, Marchand was found to have slipped away from Dresden. Bach not only won the contest by default but gave a brilliant recital to celebrate his victory, vindicating his reputation for supremacy at the keyboard.

Returning to Weimar from his triumph in Dresden, he encountered a rather different reception. When appointed to Cöthen in August, Bach had petitioned the duke for release from his employment at Weimar, a petition Wilhelm Ernst refused to grant. In such circumstances it was normal to accept the refusal – as Bach's father had done in similar circumstances – or to wait patiently until the employer relented, but Bach, despite his resignation to the will of God, was not disposed to submit to the caprice of Man. Nor was he given to patient waiting once he had made up his mind to act. The petition for release was repeated, and the duke, no doubt incensed by such insolence, not only confirmed his refusal but prevented Bach's departure from Weimar by putting his Konzertmeister under arrest. The imprisonment did not last long. No doubt Wilhelm Ernst was resigned to letting Bach go, but intended to make his displeasure clear by granting leave in his own good time and on his own terms. As the court secretary put it in official minutes:

> On 6 November 1717, Bach, till now Konzertmeister and Hoforganist, was put under arrest in the justice room for obstinately demanding his instant demission. He was released on 2 December with a grudging permission to retire from the duke's service.

We can read the composer's character very clearly in those words 'obstinately' and 'instant' – and the duke's in that 'grudging permission'.

Although Bach was to spend only six years at Cöthen out of a professional career lasting almost fifty, they were among his most productive. They were also creatively decisive, not least because the composer developed a profound rapport with Prince Leopold. The relationship between patron and artist has often been significant in the history of music, never more so than at Cöthen. Bach was as sturdily self-reliant a character as it is possible to imagine, but the strongest creative temperament may need a favourable environment in which to work. To be favourable does not mean, of course, that the environment need necessarily be pleasant: on the contrary, for certain natures, adversity can be more stimulating than pleasure and success. Bach was neither stimulated nor discouraged by adversity: he ploughed firmly on through all circumstances. But what he required to give of his best was a combination of demanding labour, disciplined routine and high esteem. A tireless worker of incomparable technical ability, he needed to be challenged and rewarded but not cosseted. This combination of factors he found in the early years at both Weimar and Leipzig and for most of his time at Cöthen, and it is not surprising that Bach expected to spend the rest of his life there.

The prince was not only a generous master, but a staunch admirer and a real friend, insofar as friendship could exist in the eighteenth century between prince and commoner. He held Bach in the greatest affection and regard, and the feeling was mutual. Leopold seems to have been lively, impulsive and somewhat extravagant, perhaps in reaction against his steady, thrifty parents. His portrait suggests an open, artistic and even romantic nature and his behaviour sometimes suggests the spoilt child. He was certainly a talented musician who sang and played the violin, viola da gamba and clavier with professional skill. As Bach himself remarked, Leopold 'not only loved but *knew* music', and it seems likely that several of the composer's Cöthen works, such as the sonatas for viola da gamba, were written for the prince to play.

If there were not quite the facilities at Cöthen provided by the duke of Weimar's wealth, any shortcomings were more than made up for by Leopold's enthusiasm and his determination to make the court a centre of musical excellence. To assist this process, he constructed a theatre in the castle orangery and the band took part in performances there. He also set about buying good instruments for the newly formed *collegium musicum* (as he called his Kapelle), dispatching Bach to Berlin to test a new harpsichord. If Bach, for lack of space

Prince Leopold of Anhalt-Cöthen, Bach's friend and admirer. Contemporary pastel portrait.

A court musician with instruments. Detail of a painting by P. J. Horemans, 1722.

elsewhere, at first had to conduct rehearsals over a shop in the town belonging to one Herr Lautsch, and then in his own house (for which he was paid twelve thalers per annum extra), he too made up for any shortcomings with enthusiasm and extraordinary creative energy. Though he may not have known the exact sums involved, he must have been well aware that Leopold was spending a substantial proportion of his income on music – an impressive practical demonstration of the prince's commitment to the art.

Bach's energy was not confined to Cöthen. Like Wilhelm Ernst, Leopold gave his Kapellmeister frequent periods of leave, and Bach made full use of them to visit fellow musicians and other courts at Leipzig, Schleiz, Zerbst, Weissenfels and elsewhere. He also accompanied his employer on formal visits and holidays. Leopold liked to include musicians in his entourage when he travelled. This allowed him to indulge his passion for music wherever he went, and provided public evidence of his own importance. Like most of his fellow rulers, great and small, Leopold had a complex network of cousins. Visiting them with his suite served the double purpose of providing pleasure and enhancing prestige. These visits were taken seriously. Only the best musicians from the band accompanied the prince, and Bach's harpsichord went along with him, cared for by no fewer than three specially deputed servants.

The time and energy required for travel, on top of all Bach's other duties, was considerable. Despite this, he produced an extraordinary volume of work in his Cöthen years, even by eighteenth-century standards, and the palace library was well stocked with his scores. The music written at Cöthen includes many 'sets' of compositions: the three solo partitas and three solo sonatas for violin, the flute sonatas, the six sonatas for violin and harpsichord, the violin concertos, the orchestral suites in C and D, the three viola da gamba sonatas and the six cello suites. There is also a great deal of keyboard music, again arranged in sets, notably the six French Suites which were probably begun in Weimar and completed in Cöthen. On 22 January 1720, he began to assemble the *Clavier-Büchlein vor Wilhelm Friedemann Bach* for his eldest son, then nine years old and a very promising clavier player. The collection included, among other things, the two-part and three-part Inventions. These pieces, and many others like them, arose from his teaching. As C. P. E. Bach later told Forkel: when gifted pupils began to lose patience after months of practising finger exercises, Bach

> was so obliging as to write little connected pieces in which those exercises were combined together. Of this kind are the six little *Preludes for Beginners* and still more the fifteen two-part *Inventions*. He wrote both down during the hours of teaching and, in doing so, attended only to the momentary want of the scholar. But he afterwards transformed them into beautiful, expressive little works of art.

For similarly pedagogic reasons, Bach may also have completed in Cöthen the six keyboard Partitas he began in Weimar, and during 1721 he put together Book I of the *Well-tempered Clavier*, a sequence of twenty-four preludes and fugues in all the major and minor keys. Many of the pieces in this collection had been composed earlier. By collecting them in this way, Bach combined his passion for order and completeness with the didactic purpose of showing how pieces in all the different keys could be played on one keyboard instrument by tuning (or 'tempering') the notes of the scale equally. In so doing, he made a characteristic intervention in a fraught contemporary debate.

In the natural scale, all the different notes are tuned at distinct pitches, so that C sharp and D flat (for example), sounded by the same key on a modern keyboard, are actually quite different from one another. But a keyboard which accommodated such differences would be unmanageable. Modulation from one tonality to another would also become problematic. Seventeenth-century musicians usually solved these problems by preferring certain keys to others and avoiding difficult key-changes, but as music became more complex such solutions could no longer suffice. In order to accommodate the full range of keys and scales, 'equal temperament' was gradually adopted, ironing out differences of natural pitch in favour of an artificial system which simplified the scale and facilitated modulation. However, this system was still controversial in Bach's time – indeed, it was not fully adopted until the mid-nineteenth century. The *Well-tempered Clavier* is therefore a formidable contribution to both the practice *and* the theory of music – and further evidence of how inseparable the two were for Bach.

But perhaps the most intriguing works of the Cöthen years are the six cello suites, which are perfect examples of the way the composer responded to the challenge of a fine player and a new medium. It is just conceivable that they were written for Prince Leopold, though their fearsome technical difficulties probably put them beyond his reach. More likely they were composed for the cellist Christian Ferdinand Abel, who joined the band at Cöthen from Berlin. Abel was the father of a more famous son, Carl Friedrich, born at Cöthen during Bach's time there, and later his pupil at Leipzig. In 1759 Carl Friedrich was to settle in London, where he continued the family connection by collaborating with Johann Christian Bach in promoting subscription concerts in that city from 1764 to 1784.

The players in the Cöthen band included three violinists, two flautists, two trumpeters, an oboist, a cellist, a bassoonist, a violist, a timpanist, an organist, and three 'ripienists' i.e., accompanists. This make-up is itself a guide to the music Bach was composing – for, like Haydn and Mozart, he was someone who exploited the resources to hand. For all except the timpanist, Bach composed both solo and ensemble music, but the supreme works these forces helped to produce are the six Brandenburg Concertos (BWV1046–51), probably begun at Weimar, but completed at Cöthen some time before March 1721. The concertos take their name from a dedication to the margrave of Brandenburg, to whom they were presented on the occasion of his forty-fourth birthday. It seems likely that Bach was introduced to the margrave when he visited Berlin to buy a harpsichord for Prince Leopold – presumably the instrument which figures so brilliantly in the fifth Brandenburg Concerto.

These works are not only superb examples of the Italian *concerto grosso* form popular at the time, in which a main body of instruments is contrasted with a smaller group; they also look forward to the solo works of a later era, especially the remarkable fifth concerto, with its enormous harpsichord cadenza. When the Cöthen band could not supply soloists, opportunities arose from the many musicians who visited the town, attracted by the new musical establishment – and of course by the presence of Bach himself. So it was that the horn players in Brandenburg no. 2 were recruited from outside, as recorded in the court register for 6 June 1722, which mentions a payment of fifteen thalers to two *Waldhornisten*.

Concerto for keyboard, with flutes, violins, horns and cello. Engraving by J. R. Holzhalb, 1777.

Waldhornists were not the only visitors. In the spring of 1719 Bach narrowly missed meeting Handel, who visited Halle where his mother still lived. Cöthen was only twenty miles from Halle, and on hearing the news of Handel's presence Bach immediately set off to meet him, but it was not to be. By the time he arrived, Handel had left for England. Bach's eagerness for the meeting and Handel's apparent indifference vividly illustrate the difference in status between the two men. Count von Flemming, who had arranged the contest between Marchand and Bach and who doubtless dreamed of an encounter between the two giants of German music, had no more success than Bach. As he wrote to one of that master's pupils:

> I tried to get a word with Mr Handel, and to pay him some civility for your sake, but I could accomplish nothing. I used your name in my invitation to him to come and see me, but he was always out or else ill. *Il est un peu fou là, ce qu'il me semble.*

George Frideric Handel (1685–1759) engraved by W. Bromley after T. Hudson, c. 1756.

One wonders whether Flemming had a reputation as a tiresome lion-hunter, to be avoided at all costs, but Handel was anyway far too grand to have to bother with importunate acquaintances, however aristocratic. If Bach was a national celebrity, Handel was by now an international star. The contrast between these exact contemporaries is striking. For all his periodic financial and artistic crises, Handel was his own man. Certainly, he depended on royal and aristocratic patrons such as George I and the duke of Chandos, but he owed far more to the wider public who flocked to his concerts and operas. Sturdily independent though he was, Bach passed his entire life in service to employers, bound like any craftsman by powerful contractual obligations. These obligations were light when, as at Cöthen, the master recognized his bondsman's supreme quality. Elsewhere they could be invoked in the most humiliating way.

Yet even Cöthen was not the earthly paradise it seemed at first. Within three years Bach was thinking of leaving. To explain his premature departure we need to look at a series of events involving marriage. First, the death of his own wife, Maria Barbara in 1720. In May of that year, Prince Leopold visited the spa town of Carlsbad, taking a small group of musicians with him, and remaining there until July. While Bach was away, his wife sickened; by the time he arrived home, Maria Barbara was dead and buried. No one knows why Bach did not return in time to be with his wife on her deathbed. They were such a devoted couple that this cannot have been deliberate. It seems probable that she was taken ill suddenly and died almost at once, too soon for her husband to be summoned.

After a marriage lasting thirteen years, she left behind her four children: Catharina Dorothea, almost twelve, Wilhelm Friedemann, not quite ten, Carl Philipp Emanuel, six, and Johann Gottfried Bernhard, five. How Bach managed with these children in the midst of his grief and his demanding life is not clear. It is likely that one of his many female cousins came to his aid, as was the custom in their clan. Certainly he himself did not mope, and would not have done so, even had his duties allowed it. For one thing, sudden death was very much a feature of life in the eighteenth century. For another, his own temperament inclined him to bury his grief in work. It is also the case that, to a profoundly devout man like Bach, Maria Barbara's death, however painful and shocking, had to be accepted as the will of God.

There was also the problem of his children's education to think about. Bach himself took care of their musical training, but for the rest he had to trust to the Lutheran school in Cöthen, founded by Leopold's mother. But Cöthen was a Calvinist town where the best resources were naturally allocated to Calvinist schools. As the endless trouble he took with their musical training shows, the education of his children was a serious matter for Bach. Though he was a prosperous professional he could not amass much capital wealth. Education was the one thing he could be sure of giving his children besides his love and devotion, and it was not certain that Cöthen could provide good enough facilities.

The problems of his own loneliness and his children's upbringing were solved by remarriage. Bach's new wife was Anna Magdalena Wilcke, the youngest daughter of the court trumpeter at Weissenfels. Both her parents came of musical stock, and Anna Magdalena had Thuringian blood in her veins. Born in 1701, she was trained as a singer and worked for the prince of Anhalt-Zerbst, a cousin of Prince Leopold. She had also been making occasional guest appearances at Cöthen for several years past, and was well-known to Bach. After their marriage she

The title page of Anna Magdalena's Clavierbüchlein.

continued to sing for the prince at a salary just half her husband's, which gave the couple a substantial joint income. The wedding took place on 3 December 1721, eighteen months after Maria Barbara's death, which suggests that Bach waited far longer than was normal at the time. His own father, for example, had remarried within six months of being widowed. But Johann Sebastian was a man of strong, deep feelings: however sturdy his outward demeanour, his private grieving for Maria Barbara was not to be hurried.

Bach's first marriage had been facilitated by a legacy from his uncle Tobias Lämmerhirt. His second was preceded by the death of Tobias' widow, the godmother of Johann Sebastian's eldest child. This brought him a second Lämmerhirt legacy, which he shared with his brothers and sister. Bach's portion amounted to about 500 thalers, or rather more than his annual salary. If these two legacies were omens they can be seen to have portended two happy marriages, for Anna Magdalena was to prove as good a wife as Maria Barbara – so good that Bach inscribed on the musical 'Notebook' he made for her four years later the following poem:

> Your servant, dearest maiden bride,
> Good fortune to your joy today,
> Who, in your beauteous bridal wreath
> And your handsome wedding-clothes,
> So make the heart laugh out from joy
> At your health and happiness
> That it's no wonder, if my tongue
> And breast now overflow from bliss.

One week after the wedding, on 11 December 1721, Prince Leopold himself became a husband by marrying his cousin, Princess Friederica Henrietta of Anhalt-Bernburg. This was a momentous event at the small court and preparations were made for elaborate celebrations. Before the marriage, those parts of the castle to be occupied by the married couple were extensively redecorated, and Leopold created a 'princely guard', for his new life was to be full of ceremony. The wedding itself was followed by five weeks of festivities. Leopold never did things by halves, and one consequence of his new preoccupation was less time – and less money –

for music. When the princess arrived, she turned out to be what Bach later called an 'amusa' – someone with little interest in the serious side of music and culture. She may also have been positively hostile to Bach, jealous of her husband's devotion to him: it would not be the first or last time a new wife has frozen out an old male friend or persuaded her husband to change his interests. Whatever the causes, she discouraged Leopold's musical passions and Bach felt a marked decline in his relationship with the prince. This was fatal to his commitment at Cöthen. If the prince lost interest, what was there to keep him in the town?

In spite of much happiness at Cöthen, Bach must have seen the way the wind was blowing: shortly after Maria Barbara's death, he had already put out feelers for a move. The organist of the Hamburg Jacobikirche died in September 1720 and the post was opened to competition. Eight candidates were invited to apply. Unable to take part in the trials because of commitments elsewhere, he nevertheless visited Hamburg before the auditions and played in the Catharinenkirche for his old hero J. A. Reincken, now ninety-seven years old and still active as an organist. Bach extemporized at length on the chorale tune *An Wasserflüssen Babylon* which he had heard Reincken himself varying twenty years earlier. After a performance in which he displayed all his inventiveness and technical brilliance, he received an accolade which must have touched him more than most, coming as it did from the aged master who best represented the musical tradition to which Bach himself belonged, when Reincken said 'I thought this art was dead, but I see it still lives in you.' Some scholars have suggested that on the same occasion Bach first played his great Fantasia and Fugue in G minor (BWV542) as a tribute to Reincken, because the fugue subject is based on a Dutch folk-song and Reincken was thought to be Dutch.

After hearing the other candidates, the judges decided to offer the post to Bach whose reputation made an audition unnecessary, but Bach refused it. We do not know why. Scholars have wondered whether he discovered on the spot in Hamburg drawbacks invisible from Cöthen. This seems unlikely. The most probable explanation for his refusal is that Bach was only flirting with the idea of moving. Always eager to find the most suitable sphere for his work, stimulated by new circumstances and unsettled by his wife's death, he was testing the water.

We can draw the same conclusion from the carefully composed dedication to the Brandenburg Concertos which were despatched to the margrave in March 1721 – nine months before Prince Leopold's marriage – with the following inscription:

> Monseigneur,
>
> Two years ago, when I had the honour of playing before your Royal Highness, I experienced your condescending interest in the insignificant musical talents with which heaven has gifted me, and understood your Royal Highness's gracious willingness to accept some pieces of my composition. In accordance with that condescending command, I take the liberty to present my most humble duty to your Royal Highness in these Concerti for several instruments, begging your Highness not to judge them by the standards of your own refined and delicate taste, but to seek in them rather the expression of my profound respect and obedience. In conclusion, Monseigneur, I most respectfully beg your Royal Highness to continue your gracious favour towards me, and to be assured that there is nothing I so much desire as to employ myself more worthily in your service.

The feelers Bach put out to Hamburg and Brandenburg suggest that, at just the moment when a more relaxed temperament would have settled for an easy life, whatever the minor disadvantages, he was looking about him for new opportunities. Bach is sometimes thought of as a conservative. His encounter with Reincken might seem to confirm this view. In his own time he was often seen to be a backward-looking composer because he worked to the end of his life in a chorale-based contrapuntal style which was passing out of favour. But Bach's temperament – his essential being – was active, positive and profoundly realistic: neither forward-looking nor backward-looking, neither nostalgic nor utopian. He never gave way to regret or introspection, never indulged in day-dreams of what might be. He faced circumstances and lived in the present. And because he was absolutely secure in his religious views, thoroughly trained in traditional musical skills, content with the social order, and profoundly happy in his conventional family life, he was able to experiment artistic-ally. His absolute mastery of traditional forms gave him the freedom to do with them anything he liked in ways which were always novel and exciting.

Bach did not go to Hamburg. Nor, so far as we know, did he receive even an acknowledgement from the margrave of Brandenburg for what must surely be the most magnificent birthday present in musical history. But by the time the next important post came up, he was ready to move in earnest. This time the opportunity was nearer at hand. One of Bach's first tasks, only a few days after his appointment to Cöthen in 1717, had involved travelling to Leipzig where he was invited to inspect the new Scheibe organ. This visit was arranged by the composer Johann Kuhnau, author of the celebrated *Biblical Sonatas* and Cantor of St Thomas's School in Leipzig from 1701. Unusually, the task was entrusted to Bach alone – a sign of the high esteem in which he was now held – and he produced a thorough report. The visit also gave him an opportunity to acquaint himself with conditions in Leipzig.

In June 1722, the ailing Kuhnau died, leaving a vacancy at St Thomas's. The post of Cantor involved training the school choir at St Thomas's to sing in the city churches. But the Cantor was also obliged to teach the boys ordinary school subjects and oversee their pastoral care, while at the same time supervising all musical activity in the church attached to the school, and participating generally in the musical life of the town. It was therefore a demanding, high-profile appointment with a commensurate salary. A Cantor could hope to earn in excess of 700 thalers per annum, and he might expect to become a figure of importance in musical life nationally.

A Lutheran hymn-book printed in Leipzig in 1710.

The town council drew up a list of six applicants for the post in which the leading candidate was the celebrated Georg Philipp Telemann, currently Cantor at Hamburg. Telemann was well-known in Leipzig where he had spent four years from 1701 to 1705 in various musical jobs. He was duly appointed Cantor in August. But

*The composer and organist Georg
Philipp Telemann (1681–1767)
who liked and admired Bach
and commemorated his death
in a sonnet. Acquatint by
V. D. Preisler.*

as so often in these matters, Telemann was not really after the job in
Leipzig. What he wanted was to negotiate an improvement in terms at
Hamburg where he had been in his post for little over a year. Achieving
this goal, he declined the Leipzig position and in November 1722 the
council started looking again.

Bach had not applied first time round – perhaps because he
assumed that Telemann would be appointed to the cantorate, perhaps
because Cantors were socially inferior to Kapellmeisters. But at the
second time of asking he joined in the competition with four other

short-listed candidates, including the landgrave of Hesse's Kapellmeister, Christoph Graupner – himself a former pupil at St Thomas's, a distinguished keyboard player and an enormously prolific composer with more than one thousand pieces of church music to his name. After another round of auditions and discussions in January 1723, the council chose Graupner. But Graupner hesitated, and it eventually became clear that, like Telemann before him, he was using the Leipzig appointment to improve his current conditions of service. When the landgrave of Hesse refused to release him, he cannot have been too disappointed. The refusal was accompanied by a substantial increase in salary and Graupner remained for the rest of his life in Darmstadt, where he died in 1760.

The way was thus left open for Bach, cordially recommended to the council by Graupner when he announced his withdrawal on 9 April 1723. After this, Bach's appointment became a formality and the elaborate municipal and ecclesiastical machinery of Leipzig swung into action. At a council meeting the same day it was agreed that Bach was a worthy successor to Kuhnau, and on 22 April the post was offered to him. There was just a chance that he might have refused it. On 4 April Prince Leopold's wife had died, after barely a year of marriage. With the 'amusa' in her grave, Leopold might have been expected to rediscover his old passion for music. But here again we find evidence of Bach's realism, and his need to move on. Things at Cöthen could never be as they had been; his years in the town had served their purpose. Even the evident disadvantages at Leipzig, where Bach would lose his financial security and his social status as Kapellmeister, could not change his feeling that it was time to go. On 13 April he had already received his dismissal from Prince Leopold's service.

One week later, Bach drafted a letter accepting the council's terms, including the assurance that he would not leave the town without permission. He also undertook

> not only to give instruction to classes in the ordinary way, but also to give private lessons to the students without extra recompense, and to discharge dutifully whatsoever else may be required of me.

These apparently straightforward promises were to be the source of much trouble in the future. On 5 May the composer attended a meeting of the council at which he was formally apprised of his appointment and signed the undertaking which specified his duties. On 8 May, Bach was introduced to the church consistory with his certificate of theological soundness for the post, acquired after an oral examination by one of their number. On 13 May he again appeared before the consistory. This time he made public subscription to the *Formula Concordiae*, a statement of doctrine issued in 1580 and designed to reconcile factions within the Lutheran Church. All church employees within Saxony were obliged to signify their acceptance of this document. On 22 May, two carriages and four wagons brought the Bach family and their possessions from Cöthen and they took up residence in the Cantor's house, which was part of the school building. On 30 May Bach inaugurated his duties with a performance of Cantata 75, *Die Elenden sollen essen*, at St Nicholas', the official town church; and on 1 June he was formally inducted into service at St Thomas's with a ceremony attended by representatives from the school, the council and the consistory. Conducted by their prefect, the scholars sang a piece of music at the door to welcome the dignitaries and the Cantor, and the town clerk announced the appointment. Bach was then introduced to his new colleagues who offered words of greeting. He expressed gratitude to his patrons in Leipzig, assured them of his diligence and loyalty, swore to conduct himself honourably, and promised that he would show due respect to those in authority over him. More music was sung to end the ceremony of welcome to the Thomasschule. Bach was to remain there for the rest of his life.

CHAPTER 6

The Cantor, Leipzig 1723–33

There was more to the elaborate ritual of Bach's election and induction at Leipzig than the undoubted self-importance of the officials involved. St Thomas's was an important post in an important place, as

Bach himself understood well. Founded in 1212 in association with an Augustinian monastery, reorganized in the mid-sixteenth century, and remaining on the same site from then until 1877, the school had from its inauguration provided boys with education and board, in return for which they sang in the churches and supported themselves – as Bach had done at Ohrdruf and Lüneburg – by singing at funerals and other ceremonial occasions.

The school was controlled by a Rector (headmaster) and his three subordinates, the Conrector, the Cantor and the Tertius (in order of seniority), assisted by junior masters. It was the senior of the two *Stadtschulen* – state schools – which were the only places providing subsidized education in Leipzig, its funds deriving mainly from pious legacies. The parents of other children had to find the cash for private tuition or do without. But although it had declined in the years immediately before Bach's arrival under the rule of a weak Rector, St Thomas's was still a fine school and there was competition for entry. Every candidate had to pass tests in general knowledge and musical proficiency and undertake to remain at the school for several years. When Bach arrived there were sixty-one singers, ranging in age from eleven to seventeen and divided into classes, each with its own dormitory. Fifty-five were foundation scholars.

If the school was an important institution in Leipzig, the town was a force to be reckoned with in Saxony where it was second only to the capital city of Dresden. The population – about 30,000 in Bach's time – was large enough to include a substantial professional middle class, and this gave it a quite different feel to aristocratic

The Leipzig Thomasschule and Thomaskirche, engraved in 1723.

The fine gardens and avenues of Leipzig, recorded in 1777 in an engraving by J. A. Rossmäsler.

Weimar and Cöthen. Leipzig was to middle Germany what Hamburg was to the north: a thriving commercial and financial regional centre, ultimately ruled by the elector of Saxony but administered by a council of thirty assessors and three burgomasters, elected annually in rotation. The elector's authority was represented by the governor of the fortress, manned by royal soldiers and supported by volunteers. Leipzig was by far the largest community Bach had ever worked in, which was no doubt one of its attractions. Here there were schools and a university for his children, plays and concerts for entertainment, intellectual stimulus and a lively social life in pleasure-gardens and coffee-houses. The milieu was both grand and pleasing: the main streets were broad and handsome, illuminated at night by 700 oil-lamps on oak posts, and patrolled by four night-watchmen equipped with rattles to cry the hours and guard against thieves. The main thoroughfares were also liberally provided with gutters and fountains – an important feature given the deficiencies of eighteenth-century plumbing and all its health hazards.

Communications were good. Leipzig was the centre of the regional postal service with regular coaches to Dresden, Berlin, Hanover and Hamburg which helped to give the place a metropolitan feel. It was a senior post-office official who assembled many libretti for Bach under the pen-name 'Picander', including the *St Mark* and *St Matthew* Passions. The city was also famous for its publishers, including the firm of Breitkopf and Härtel which was to be such a force in music publishing through the following centuries. This was not the only business which flourished. Since the twelfth century, trade fairs had attracted people from all over the empire, stimulating the city's prosperous commercial life. In addition, Leipzig was a judicial centre – the seat of the High Court – and an academic powerhouse, famous for its university, founded in 1409 and now staffed by twenty-nine professors. The university authorities wielded considerable power, especially where music was concerned, as Bach was to find when he became involved with one of the two music societies, or *collegia musicale*. In the 148 pages of the town directory for 1736, almost forty are devoted to listing university institutions and officials.

There was also a powerful Lutheran hierarchy, in charge of six great churches. These included the university chapel of St Paul; the church of St Thomas, attached to the school in which Bach held his appointment as Cantor; and St Nicholas', the official town church until 1755, where Bach performed cantatas on alternate Sundays. Here were great opportunities for making music in the tradition which Bach knew so intimately from his own upbringing and training. Weiss, the pastor of St Thomas's, was a good friend and, like Archdeacon Eilmar at Mühlhausen, may have provided him with texts for several cantatas. In short, by settling in Leipzig Bach was returning to his musical, social and religious roots. He must have felt at home.

Bach's private and professional lives in Leipzig are even more difficult than usual to disentangle, not least because he lived, quite literally, over the shop. The Cantor and his family were housed under the same roof as the school. Dormitories and classrooms occupied the centre of a large block next to St Thomas's Church, with the Rector's apartments on one side and the Cantor's on the other. All three had separate entrances opening onto the street but were linked by a passage on the second storey. Bach's house had two large rooms on the ground floor, probably serving as bedrooms for his sons, with a wash-house at the back. On the floor above there were two bedrooms, a dining-room, maid's room, parlour and the narrow study with one window in which Bach composed. On the second floor were further bedrooms and a door opening from the Cantor's house to the school practice-room. The back of the building looked out over gardens, the river Pleisse – and a mill: performances of Bach's music in the school practice-room must often have mingled with the sound of a mill-wheel, much as Veit Bach's playing had, more than a century earlier.

After twenty years of occupation by Kuhnau and his eight children, of whom four remained with him at his death, the house needed considerable refurbishment before Bach and his family could occupy it. A mason, a joiner, a carpenter and a locksmith worked on the site for several months. The council installed a new oven weighing two and a quarter hundredweights in the kitchen, and employed a charlady, Eva Klemm, to scrub and clean for a week before the walls were white-

Three engravings of contemporary instrument makers by Christoph Weigel, 1698.

washed. Eight years after Bach arrived in Leipzig the school building was reconstructed to provide more space for the boys. The roof was removed and two storeys added, providing seven floors altogether. But the Cantor's house remained as it had been, so four of the school floors now stretched above it. Bach's quarters were therefore surrounded by children's bedrooms, domestic offices and school dormitories, while his study was separated from the junior classrooms next to it only

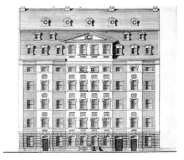

The Thomasschule after enlargement, 1732.

by a thin lath-and-plaster partition. The noise and bustle must often have been considerable, yet there is no sign that he was in any way distracted from his work.

This is not surprising. Bach did not require romantic solitude, and thrived on active life. Even so, the Cantor's house was very full indeed. Johann Sebastian and Anna Magdalena continued to produce children at yearly intervals. Many died in infancy, but the five survivors shared their lodging with a maid, the usual complement of pupils and Bach's older children, and there might be twelve people living in the house and many more coming and going. The three sons from his first marriage were enrolled at the Thomasschule where they sang in the choir and did well academically. Wilhelm Friedemann, in particular, was not merely a very talented musician but a clever, lively boy; his school notebooks reveal him as both amusing and easily bored, with a taste for drawing caricatures in the margin. As soon as the family arrived in Leipzig, young 'Friede's' father entered him for eventual matriculation at the university. Bach was devoted to his eldest son. They attended the opera in Dresden together, and Johann Sebastian took the greatest pains with his musical education, in 1726 sending him away for a year to learn the violin with a pupil of Tartini.

Life at school was not easy, to begin with. Bach got on well with the elderly Rector, Johann Heinrich Ernesti, but Ernesti was more interested

A page from Wilhelm Friedemann's school notebook.

in his professorship of poetry at Leipzig University than in the school. Appointed Rector in 1684 – the year before Bach was born – he had more or less lost control of discipline by the 1720s. The school buildings, erected in 1554, had deteriorated badly, and the boys were even more fractious and difficult to control because of their cramped and uncomfortable conditions. Some slept two to a bed, and the school dining-room doubled as accommodation for three classes. Heating and ventilation were minimal, illness was common, and one can deduce the perils of life at St Thomas's from the fact that the school rules provided for younger boys to hear the Sunday sermon in school if the inspector decided that the church was too cold to endure.

Pupils were also overworked. Besides their lessons and their duties in church they were expected to follow and sing at every funeral, except pauper burials, whatever the weather. From New Year's Day to mid-January they sang in the streets for charitable contributions. Their day lasted from five or six o'clock in the morning to seven or eight at night, according to the season, and long church services meant little rest on Sundays. Holidays were brief.

Bach, too, was overworked. The school statutes required masters to teach for up to four hours a day, or to provide substitutes at their own expense. Most of Bach's non-musical classes were eventually taken over by the Tertius, Herr Pezold, for fifty thalers per annum. This arrangement relieved him in the short term but stored up trouble for the future when Pezold was found to be incompetent and Bach was blamed for his failings. Even so, in addition to training singers and maintaining discipline in the choir, Bach still had to teach Luther's Latin Catechism once a week and to participate in monthly inspections, staff meetings, rehearsals, town ceremonies and church services. Then he had to find time for composing. But find it he did. In his first decade at Leipzig, he produced six trio sonatas and other works for organ, concertos and orchestral suites, several Passions, oratorios and motets, hundreds of cantatas, and doubtless a good deal of music now lost.

But the regular focal point of his work was the Sunday service in the churches of St Thomas and St Nicholas. Weekday devotions in the Lutheran rite involved the minimum of music: hymns sung by small choirs provided from the school. But on Sunday there was a full choral service in both churches, the *Hauptgottesdienst*, which began at 7.0 a.m. and lasted until mid-day. Except during Lent and Advent, a cantata was performed every Sunday by the main choir (*chorus primus*) from St Thomas's in one church under Bach's own direction, while the other choir (the *chorus secundus*)

The Nikolaikirche organ. Watercolour by K. B. Schwartz, before 1785.

sang a simpler version of the service in the other church under his deputy. The two churches alternated cantata performances throughout the year, though Bach much preferred to perform in St Thomas's, which had two organs and two galleries large enough to accommodate a double choir of the sort used in the *St Matthew Passion*.

Cantatas were also required for feast-days, which meant that Bach had to perform a cycle of fifty-nine cantatas through the year. In addition he was obliged to provide Passion music, a Magnificat and motets for the funeral services of prosperous citizens. While some of this music could be recycled from older works, there was a constant demand for new material – so constant that during his first years at Leipzig, and in addition to all his other duties, he appears to have composed on average *one cantata per week*. Carl Philipp Emanuel Bach told Forkel that his father produced five complete sequences of cantatas for the liturgical year. It now appears he may actually have composed 'only' three cycles, the others drawing on pre-existing material. Scholars are still arguing over the matter. Even so, it is an astonishing achievement. Though the quantity is not unusual for Bach's time – the indefatigable Telemann is thought to have composed more than two thousand cantatas – the quality is uniquely and uniformly high.

The sheer scale of music-making in Leipzig brought other problems with it, for Bach was not only Cantor but also 'Director Musices', in which capacity he provided music for city celebrations, royal visits and feast-day services at the university church. On such occasions he had at his disposal a small body of professional musicians which he dryly enumerated in 1730 as 'Four town pipers, three professional fiddlers, and one apprentice. Modesty forbids me to speak at all truthfully of their qualities and musical knowledge.' In addition, he could also draw on instrumentalists in the choir – though this meant depleting the body of singers – and students from the university. Despite these comparatively meagre and often undependable resources, the choral works he wrote

'The Cantor'. Engraving by Christoph Weigel, 1698.

in such quantities at Leipzig display an astonishing variety of instrumental colour. One of his first major works for Leipzig, the *St John Passion* (BWV245), first performed on Good Friday 1724, is a magnificent example. Though the earlier work is often counted inferior to the *St Matthew Passion* (BWV244), nothing could excel the opening chorus in splendour.

The Passions are now among the most popular works by Bach. Only two have survived from a possible total of five, but these two represent the high point of a German musical tradition which stretches back to the Middle Ages, when the story of the Crucifixion was told each Easter in unaccompanied plainsong settings. These settings themselves derive from more ancient practices, possibly dating back as far as the fourth century, when a priest would recite the Gospel story of Christ's Passion during Holy Week. By the twelfth century the performance involved three clergy, now singing: a tenor Narrator, a bass Christ and alto Crowd. Over time, the setting became more sophisticated. During the sixteenth century the plainchant narrative was regularly interspersed with polyphonic choruses, the text in reformed churches was translated into the vernacular, and Lutheran Passions appealed directly to the congregation by including chorale tunes. These changes gradually shifted the emphasis of Passions from simple narrative to complex drama.

The form continued to develop in the seventeenth century, notably in the music of Heinrich Schütz, who worked for many years in Dresden. Schütz is credited with composing the first German opera, and his experience in the opera house must have influenced his superbly dramatic Passion settings in which the choir is accompanied by strings, further characters are brought into the story, and plainsong is replaced by Italianate recitative. Other composers introduced reflective choruses and arias and replaced the Gospel text with a metrical paraphrase. Devout congregations were often scandalized by such innovations which seemed to bring the theatre into the church, but these were the traditions which Bach inherited and perfected in his own sublime Passions.

Producing music of this quality in such quantity might have been enough for most men, but Bach was keen to assert his status as Director Musices, however much extra labour it involved. The Leipzig director of music was in effect a kind of Kapellmeister and, as the years passed, Bach increasingly saw himself as composer and performer, not as choirmaster. It was this preference which contributed to many later difficulties at Leipzig, eventually bringing him into conflict with his employers. For, as Bach was soon to discover, the city was ruled by competing oligarchies, each with a beady eye on its own sphere of influence. Because the lines between school, church, council and university were not clearly drawn, there were endless petty disputes between them – and between them and their employees – about who should do what. In Weimar one petty tyrant blighted the lives of his subjects; in Leipzig the tyrants were many and at loggerheads.

This became apparent as soon as Bach arrived. For his installation as Cantor, the consistory had requested the pastor of St Thomas's, Christian Weiss, to welcome him in their name. The council took exception to this move, claiming that it was for them to welcome the Cantor and that the church had never before taken such a part in the ceremony. The argument began immediately and continued in the sort of lengthy nit-picking correspondence which was to be typical of Bach's years at Leipzig.

The trouble was implicit in his terms of employment, for the post of Cantor involved several different but closely related duties. Within the Thomasschule itself he had to approve suitable candidates for admission to the upper school, train them in instrumental and vocal music, apply appropriate discipline when necessary, teach other subjects as agreed, and generally supervise their education and their behaviour while maintaining musical and academic standards. The question of standards was of urgent practical importance, because the Cantor was charged to ensure that the music provided was well-performed and 'neither too lengthy nor operatic in style, but such as shall encourage the congregation to true devotion and reverence in church'. He also supervised the work of the organists and other musicians in the two churches and was expected to furnish scores and parts for their performances. If there were musical problems, in short, he was held to be responsible.

Nor was his post at St Thomas's merely supervisory or managerial. Bach was involved in the normal menial duties of a boarding-school master. Each weekday there were lessons to be taught and at twelve noon he met the upper school for choir practice. Every fourth week he was obliged by his contract to act as school inspector, which meant rousing the boys at 5.0 a.m., taking morning and evening prayers, presiding at meals and administering discipline. This was a far cry from the lofty elegance of court life at Cöthen.

In addition to his work in school and church, there were pieces to be composed for the many civic ceremonies which took place in this proud

The Jena Collegium Musicum holding an audition. Watercolour, 1740.

city, including the annual installation of the council, the elector's visits and other state occasions. Then there were private or semi-private functions at which the choristers and their Cantor earned fees, especially the weddings and funerals of wealthy citizens. This was an important matter for Bach himself, as the fees formed the most substantial if fluctuating part of his income at Leipzig, far larger than his basic salary as Cantor. Though his yearly income might amount to 700 thalers – a considerable increase on his Cöthen emoluments – only a fraction of this was regular.

Matters were further complicated by Bach's uncertain standing in the city. The warm personal relationship between musician and employer he had experienced in Cöthen, and even at first in Weimar, was entirely lacking. And a Cantor, however grand, was considered socially and professionally inferior to a Kapellmeister. The move to Leipzig was therefore a step downwards. Although direct comparisons are hard to make, in today's terms one might say it was the difference between directing music in a great school and conducting a famous orchestra. There is plenty of evidence that Bach minded about such distinctions. With Prince Leopold's consent, he continued to style himself Kapellmeister until that prince's death in 1728, after which he managed to secure the title of *Hofcomponist* – court composer – from the duke of Saxe-Weissenfels and waged a long campaign to extract the same honour from the elector of Saxony. And although he was a first-rate teacher, Bach was unwilling to become a mere schoolmaster. As if to show this, he insisted in all official dealings and documents on his title as Director Musices, which he considered to underline his status as musical overlord of the whole town.

The strategy might have worked had the town not included a university with which he was soon embroiled in a very characteristic row about who should direct music in the university chapel of St Paul's. This was traditionally the privilege of the Thomascantor but, in the interval between Kuhnau's death and the installation of his successor, the university had appointed its own director of music, one J. G. Görner. This encroachment on the new Cantor's rights was aggravated by the fact that Görner also chanced to be his deputy as organist at St Nicholas'. Bach tried to regain musical control of St Paul's but the university authorities stood firm. After months of inconclusive wrangling – and too many tactless remarks about Görner's lack of talent – he took his case to Dresden, presenting the elector with no fewer than three petitions about the matter, the last a closely argued document of three thousand words. But the Cantor was no match for academics when it came to squabbling over contracts, and although the elector conceded Bach's right to direct certain long-established services at St Paul's, he decreed that the university could otherwise do as it liked.

Once this affair was settled in the winter of 1726, Bach seemed to lose interest in St Paul's altogether – until, that is, another cause of rancour arose. The elector's wife, Christiane Eberhardine, died in September 1727; as an act of homage to this popular princess, an aristocratic university student, Hans Carl von Kirchbach, offered to subsidize a memorial service for her at St Paul's, during which he proposed to read an oration.

The poet Johann Christoph Gottsched – also a professor at the university – was commissioned to write a funeral ode for Bach to set to music. But when the university authorities heard of this, they objected to Kirchbach's choice and insisted that Görner receive the commission, as university director of music. Replying that Bach had already completed his task, Kirchbach was then told that Görner – and most definitely not Bach – would at least direct the performance, upon which Kirchbach threatened to abandon the enterprise altogether. After much argument a compromise was agreed: Görner was to receive a present of twelve thalers from Kirchbach, while Bach was required to sign a disclaimer promising that he would not consider the occasion a precedent for the future. In the event, Görner got his money but Bach refused to sign. Despite his refusal, on 17 October Cantata 198, known as the *Trauer Ode*, was performed – with its composer in charge at the harpsichord.

The music of Cantata 198 is very fine. Significantly, it is in the key of B minor, which had a particularly expressive resonance for Bach. The words, too, are of higher quality than usual. Though by no means a great poet, Gottsched was a more distinguished figure than most of Bach's librettists. Strongly influenced by French Classicism, he was a celebrated critic and intellectual who exerted considerable influence on the growing German Enlightenment, and his verse is lucid, dignified and austere. These qualities, together with the genuine public grief for Christiane Eberhardine, may have helped to elicit such magnificent music from Bach, who later drew on it for the *St Mark Passion*, performed in 1731 but now lost. The *Trauer Ode* certainly articulates more than merely ceremonial mourning. The constant use of repeated notes and falling octaves in the bass line, for example, gives the music a peculiarly sombre colouring, as though funeral bells were tolling throughout. This effect is strikingly evoked by the most unusual use of two lutes in the fourth recitative, where the text refers explicitly to bells and the lutes mimic their chiming.

Having alienated the university authorities, Bach then proceeded to estrange the church and council leaders, who were already displeased with him. Indeed, time and again his lack of diplomacy was to aggravate petty disagreements – one with the subdeacon at St Nicholas', for example, about who should choose the hymns for Vespers. As any reader of Anthony Trollope will know, ecclesiastical establishments are fertile ground for bitter quarrels about trifling matters, and church music has often been one of the bones of contention. Like many musicians in such circumstances, before and since, Bach's professional perfectionism and personal stubbornness blinded him to the sensibilities of others.

But some of those others were well-placed to exact their revenge. In May 1729, Bach conducted his annual examination of candidates for admission to St Thomas's, and sent to the council a detailed list of his conclusions. The report was countersigned by the Rector, Ernesti, but the councillors declined to accept it. Clearly signalling their determination to put Bach in his place, they rejected many candidates he had approved, accepting four he had found unsuitable and one he had not even tested. This was an affront to his professional standing and it was accompanied by a barrage of complaints about Bach's unacceptable attitude to his work.

The timing of this row was especially unfortunate. Two months earlier Bach had been obliged to perform one of the saddest duties of his life. Prince Leopold had died on 19 November 1728 at the age of only thirty-three, and in March 1729, a few weeks before the first Good Friday performance of the *St Matthew Passion* in the Thomaskirche, Bach travelled to Cöthen to attend the formal obsequies for his old friend and patron. Despite his enormous workload in Leipzig, Bach's relations with the prince had remained very warm and he had continued to write occasional music for Cöthen. In 1726, for example, he dedicated the first of the six Partitas (eventually published together in 1731 as *Clavier-Übung* I) to the child of the prince's second marriage, Emanuel Ludwig. In joint celebration of the boy's birth and publication of his own work, Bach also sent a poem in which they are united:

> To the most excellent Prince Emanuel Ludwig, Crown Prince of Anhalt, Duke of Saxony, Enger, and Westphalia, Count of Ascania, Lord of Bernburg and Zerbst, &c., &c., these trifling musical firstfruits are dedicated with sincere devotion by Johann Sebastian Bach.

Serenest
>   infant Prince,
>>   whom swaddling bands encumber,
Although thy princely glance declares maturer age,
Forgive me if I dare to wake thee from thy slumber,
And humbly crave thy grace for this my playful page.

These firstfruits of my lyre to thee I dare to bring,
Thou Prince first born to feel a mother's royal kiss,
Hoping that she to thee the lay may sometime sing;
For of her womb thou art a firstfruit too, like this.

The wiseheads fain would scare us mortals with a warning
Because into the world we come with cries and tears,
As though they could foretell the evening from the morning,
And see our future clear beyond the veil of years.

But I will answer them and say, that as these chords
That round thy cradle swell are sweet and clear and pure,
So shall thy life flow on through all that earth affords
Of harmony and joy, calm, happy, and secure.

May I, most hopeful Prince, play for thy delectation,
When thousandfold thy powers exceed what men now mark!
I pray, for my own part, for constant inspiration,
And am,
>   most noble Prince,
>>   thy
>>>   humble servant,
>>>>   Bach.

Sadly, the child's life did not 'flow on' and he predeceased his father by several months. Bach was accompanied to Prince Leopold's funeral by Anna Magdalena and Wilhelm Friedemann. His cantata for the occasion (now lost, but probably drawing heavily on the music of his new *St Matthew Passion*) was rewarded with the enormous sum of 230 thalers – a posthumous testament to Leopold's enduring respect and affection. This must have brought home to him the difference between his misery at Leipzig and his former happiness at Cöthen – not least because the loss of a true friend was compounded by the further loss of Bach's role as honorary Cöthen Kapellmeister, a title which lapsed with Leopold's death.

Events at Cöthen can only have exacerbated his irritation with the councillors of Leipzig, who were in turn becoming increasingly annoyed with Bach. Astonishingly, as it must seem to us now, the *St Matthew Passion* appears to have made no impression on them. All they could think about were what they saw as their Cantor's contractual shortcomings. The value the composer put on this work is clear from the beautifully written manuscript he produced, in which the biblical words of the Evangelist are written in red ink to distinguish them from the rest of the text by Bach's friend Picander. This manuscript is an extraordinary achievement, given the pressure of Bach's other obligations. Like the work itself, it seems to indicate Bach's personal sympathy with Matthew's version of the Gospel story, which emphasizes the human drama of the Passion more than its theological meaning. The composer's personal devotion to his Saviour is movingly apparent, and the music is characterized by the strongest, deepest and tenderest feelings.

The sublimity of these feelings makes a grotesque and painful contrast with the petty quarrels between Cantor and councillors which rumbled on through 1729 and the following year, reaching a climax in August 1730, when Bach's failings were discussed and extensively minuted at a council meeting because of complaints about his deputy, Pezold, who was turning out to be a most inadequate teacher. Bach was said by hostile councillors to take frequent absences without permission, to neglect his choir practices and generally to conduct himself in an unseemly way. He was described as lazy and incorrigible, and his critics complained of his repeated insolence in refusing even to answer the charges against him. In consequence they resolved to reduce his salary by restricting his fees. It was a rerun of the Arnstadt troubles of twenty-five years earlier.

Soon after this acrimonious meeting, Bach fired off a letter to the authorities, dated 23 August 1730. In it, he outlines *their* obligations to *him* in what he calls 'A short but indispensable sketch of what constitutes a well-appointed church music'. This memorandum examines the practicalities of music-making in Leipzig; it is, indeed, a major source for our understanding of musical life in the city. But it also contains intriguing

Bird's-eye view of the Market Square, Leipzig, with Town Hall (centre). Engraving by J. G. Schreiber, 1712.

general reflections on contemporary music which throw considerable light on misconceptions about Bach's attitude to musical fashion.

> Now the present *status Musices* is quite different from what it was, its technique is so much more complex, and the public *gusto* so changed, that old-fashioned music sounds strangely in our ears. Greater care must therefore be taken to obtain *subjecta* capable of satisfying the modern *gustum* in music, and also instructed in its technique, to say nothing of the composer's desire to hear his works performed properly. Yet the *beneficia*, themselves inconsiderable, formerly available for the *chorus musicus*, have been withdrawn. It is astonishing that German musicians should be expected to play *ex tempore* any music put before them, whether it comes from Italy, France, England or Poland, just as if they were the *virtuosi* for whom it was written, men who therefore have had opportunity to study it, indeed almost to learn it by heart, enjoy (*quod notandum*) large salaries to reward their labour and diligence, and have leisure to study and master their parts ... let anyone visit Dresden and observe how the royal musicians are paid. They have no anxiety regarding their livelihood, and consequently are relieved of *chagrin*; each man is able to cultivate his own instrument and to make himself a competent and agreeable performer on it ...

The first lines of Bach's 1730 memorandum to Leipzig Council.

Given the extravagant politeness with which employees normally addressed employers at the time – evident in the dedication of the Brandenburg Concertos, for example – the 1730 memorandum is a blunt document. Nor were the tactless comparisons between Leipzig and Dresden likely to endear its author to the councillors. Naturally conservative, they appear here as negative reactionaries, while Bach presents himself as modern and enlightened, completely *au fait* with musical fashion. There is also a strong hint of irony from one who was well capable – and notoriously so – of playing at sight almost any music put before him.

While this letter makes Bach's dissatisfaction with conditions at Leipzig eminently clear, he may have had another motive for writing it. In October 1729, while Bach was quarrelling with the council, J. H. Ernesti died after forty-five years as Rector of the Thomasschule. His death had unpleasant immediate consequences for the Cantor, because it gave the council an excuse to vent their spleen by increasing his school duties during the interregnum between rectors, without paying him extra salary. To drive the point home, at the same time they increased by one hundred per cent the stipend of Herr Gerlach, who had been appointed to the New Church at Bach's recommendation. By stating his needs so firmly and so comprehensively in his letter to the council, Bach may have hoped to strengthen his position with a new Rector. Given the state of the place, physically and morally, any incomer was bound to make sweeping changes, and here was an opportunity to put in a claim for music – which the school, after all, was supposedly founded to promote.

As it turned out, the new appointment proved to be fortunate for Bach, when an old friend from Weimar days, the philologist J. M. Gesner, took up the post in September 1730. Born in 1691, Johann Matthias Gesner became librarian and Conrector of the school at Weimar in 1715. In 1729 he was appointed Rector of the school at Ansbach, his birthplace, but promotion and professional ambition brought him to Leipzig within a year. With his high reputation as a classical scholar, Gesner also expected to follow Ernesti in the professorial chair of poetry at Leipzig University, but it is a sign of just how run-down and unruly the Thomasschule had become that the council declined to allow this, on the grounds that the school required his full-time attention.

For once they were right. Gesner made a deeply favourable impression on his colleagues by taking school discipline firmly in hand straight away. The new disciplinary code he drew up makes it clear what sort of problems he faced. Intentional mistakes in singing were to be severely corrected and even blunders punished. Boys were fined fixed amounts for certain crimes and whipped for others. Each class was assigned to a dormitory, which was governed by a distinct set of regulations thought appropriate to the age of the boys. The tariff of fines in *Sexta* – the sixth class – went as follows:

1	For losing the key or leaving it in the door	*4 gr.
2	For failing to shut the door when last to leave	2 gr.
3	For being sick	2 gr.
4	For swearing, noisy or improper speech	6 pf.
5	For rude language in Latin or German	6 pf.
6	For not getting up in the morning and missing prayers	3 pf.
7	For not tidying the cubicle by the allotted time	6 pf.

* 10 pfennigs = 1 groschen, approx. 30 groschen = 1 thaler.

But the harshness of the discipline matched the potential rowdiness of the life. Smoking and drinking were not uncommon, older pupils were known to take long absences without permission, and fighting was a common hazard among lively boys – many of them really young men – penned up together in cramped quarters.

Though strict, Gesner was nevertheless a kind and friendly man who took a genuine interest in his pupils, reading their weekly diaries and even listening to their rehearsals. Believing passionately in the importance of music in education – not always the case among choir-school head-masters – he became one of Bach's staunchest admirers. In a footnote to his edition of Quintilian's *Institutes*, published in 1738, Gesner was to leave a comparison of the composer with the musicians of antiquity which is both portrait and assessment. His words show how closely – and with what affection – he must have observed Bach.

You would think but slightly, my dear Fabius, of all these, if, returning from the underworld, you could see Bach (to mention him particularly, since he was not long ago my colleague at the Leipzig Thomasschule), either playing our clavier, which is many citharas in one, with all the fingers of both hands, or running over the keys of the instrument of instruments, whose innumerable pipes are brought to life by bellows, with both hands and, at the utmost speed, with his feet, producing by himself the most various and at the same time mutually agreeable combinations of sounds in orderly procession. If you could see him, I say, doing what many of your citharoedists and six hundred of your tibia players together could not do, not only, like a citharoedist, singing with one voice and playing his own parts, but watching over everything and bringing back to the rhythm and the beat, out of thirty or even forty musicians, the one with a nod, another by tapping with his foot, the third with a warning finger, giving the right note to one from the top of his voice, to another from the bottom, and to a third from the middle of it – all alone, in the midst of the greatest din made by all the participants, and, although he is executing the most difficult parts himself, noticing at once whenever and wherever a mistake occurs, holding everyone together, taking precautions everywhere, and repairing any unsteadiness, full of rhythm in every part of his body – this one man taking in all these harmonies with his keen ear and emitting with his voice alone the tone of all the voices. Favourer as I am of antiquity, the accomplishments of our Bach, and of any others that there may be like him, appear to me to effect what not many Orpheuses, nor twenty Arions, could achieve.

Recognizing his Cantor's unhappiness, Gesner soon took action to improve things. He released Bach from even the nominal obligation to teach non-musical subjects and instead put him in charge of attendance at weekday services. The death of Bach's deputy, Pezold, in May 1731, just six months after Gesner's arrival, smoothed the way for this change, and the new Rector also persuaded the council to restore the fees they had stopped paying Bach.

Gesner was able to present these innovations as part of a far-reaching programme of reform at the school, including a complete reconstruction of the overcrowded buildings which added two storeys to the Thomasschule. In June 1732, rebuilding was completed, the family moved back into their house, and Bach composed music (now lost) for the ceremonial reopening.

Gesner also rose to the challenge implicit in Bach's letter by reasserting the role of music in his redrafting of school regulations, published by Breitkopf in 1733. The art of music, Gesner wrote, linked its performers with the heavenly choir, and the boys should be prepared to sacrifice even their leisure hours for such a privilege. A subtle observer might have inferred from the very need to make such an assertion, that the founding purpose of the school – providing music for Leipzig – no longer held, but for the moment Bach was content.

In fact, for all his grumbling – which seems to have been as much caused by constitutional need as by real problems – the early 1730s were very good years for Bach. In the spring of 1729, amidst all his disputes with authority, he had succeeded Georg Balthasar Schott as director of the collegium musicum founded by Telemann in 1702. This was a considerable step towards achieving his aim of becoming more a Kapellmeister than a Cantor. There were two such music societies in the town, the other directed by the organist at the Thomaskirche, the ubiquitous J. G. Görner. Both involved university students and professional musicians, including Bach's own sons. His collegium musicum met on Friday evenings in Zimmerman's Coffee-House. Weather permitting, they played in the garden. Their performances were in effect public concerts, and Bach continued to direct them until he began to withdraw from musical life in the early 1740s.

His new post appears to have stimulated him to produce instrumental music again, after the strenuous years devoted to cantata cycles. Orchestral Suites nos. 2 and 4 and most of the surviving harpsichord concertos appeared in the 1730s. In 1731 he engraved and published his opus one, the first *Clavier-Übung*, the set of six Partitas referred to earlier. In retrospect, it seems amazing that Bach should have waited so long before engaging in formal publication of his music, though there were of course already many handwritten copies of his work available. In homage to his predecessor – and perhaps to make the point that he was now no longer working in Kuhnau's shadow – he took the terms 'partita' and 'clavier-übung' from that master. According to Forkel, the publication was a great success, attracting universal notice. 'Such compositions for the clavier had not been seen or heard before, and anyone who could play them was sure of a success.' At the age of forty-six, Bach at last found fame as a composer.

As if to set the seal on his success in these years, his sons embarked upon their own brilliant careers. Carl Philipp Emanuel, aged seventeen, published *his* opus one in 1731, a minuet for clavier which he engraved himself. And in July 1733, at the age of twenty-two, Wilhelm Friedemann was appointed organist at the Sophienkirche in the Saxon capital city, Dresden. He was no doubt assisted by his father's reputation and discreet lobbying but the help was hardly necessary. Wilhelm Friedemann had proved to be a performer worthy of his father's name.

Bach was a frequent visitor to Dresden in the 1730s, giving organ recitals and often attending the opera where the powerful and influential Johann Adolf Hasse was in charge from 1731 until 1763. Hasse was married to the celebrated soprano Faustina Bordoni who had sung for Handel's London opera season in the 1720s. The couple were good friends of Bach's and returned his visits when they were in Leipzig. In 1733 Bach's trips to Dresden received a new impetus when Friedrich August I, elector of Saxony and king of Poland – known as Augustus the Strong – died on 1 February, to be succeeded by his son, Friederich August II.

Unlike his father, the new elector was an energetic patron of music and painting, and Bach seized the opportunity to impress him. Whenever the elector came to Leipzig, Bach conducted performances by his collegium musicum, composing new music or revising old pieces for the birthday celebrations of the monarch and his wife. The royal couple first visited Leipzig on 5 October 1734, and were received with full ceremonial. Cannons were fired at mid-day and at night the streets and squares were illuminated with festive lights. At 9.0 p.m. six hundred university students made a torchlight procession to the royal residence where Bach's colleg- ium musicum performed *Preise dein Glücke*, a ceremonial cantata with trumpets and drums. The occasion was a spectacular success, marred only by the death next day of one of the musicians, brought on, it was said, by overexertion at the performance and inhaling smoke from the torches. But this misfortune did not prevent Bach presenting his royal master with yet another cantata on 7 October, the elector's birthday.

An open-air evening concert given by the Jena Collegium Musicum. Watercolour, 1740.

One consequence of the old elector's death was a five-month period of official mourning during the spring and summer of 1733, when 'figural' music (i.e. anything more elaborate than chorales) was not performed in churches. This breathing-space left Bach free to devote himself to other projects, including composition of the Kyrie and Gloria which were to become the core of the famous Mass in B minor. It may seem curious that one of the greatest masterpieces left by this fervent Lutheran should be a setting of the Roman liturgy. So far as we know, a full setting was not Bach's original intention – though, as with everything he did, there was a very clear purpose in view for these movements when they were first composed. Bach intended to present them to the new elector in the hope of winning appointment as court composer. The late elector had converted to Catholicism in 1712 in order to secure the throne of Poland (which was itself elective). For the same reason, his son later followed suit, and duly succeeded as king of Poland after seeing off a rival candidate in January 1734. Presenting a Kyrie and Gloria was an ingenious compliment to one who ruled both Catholic and Protestant states, because these are the movements common to the Roman and Lutheran rites. It was only much later, with the addition of further sections of the liturgy, that the work became a full-blown Catholic mass. Had the elector but known it, he had already been presented with another movement from the future B minor Mass – the Osanna – as one of the choruses in *Preise den Glücke*: a striking example of the way in which Bach, like Handel, was ready to use the same music for religious and secular purposes.

Bach sent his music to Dresden on 27 July 1733, together with a very frank request for appointment to the post he coveted:

> Most gracious sovereign and illustrious Elector,
>
> With profoundest *devotion* I offer your Majesty the accompanying insignificant example of my skill in *Musique*, begging in all humility that it may be received, not as its merits as a *composition* deserve, but with your Majesty's notorious generosity. At the same time, I solicit your Majesty's powerful *protection*. For some years past I have exercised the directorium of the music in the two principal churches in Leipzig, a situation in which I have been constantly exposed to undeserved affronts, even the confiscation of the *accidentia* due to me, annoyances not likely to recur should your Majesty be pleased to admit me to your Capelle and direct a *Praedicat* to be issued to that effect by the proper authority. Your Majesty's gracious response to my humble prayer will place me under an enduring obligation, and, with the most dutiful obedience and unflagging diligence, I shall show myself ready to fulfil your Majesty's commands to compose *Musique* for church or *orchestre*, devoting all my powers to your Majesty's service.

Despite his frankness and ingenuity, Bach was not successful in his attempt to become court composer on this occasion. For that honour he had to wait another three years – by which time his career in Leipzig was once more spiralling downwards.

CHAPTER 7

The Cantor, Leipzig 1733–50

Bach's 1733 address to the elector of Saxony makes it clear that he was by no means resigned to the situation in Leipzig. Nor had he forgiven the affronts offered him. On the contrary, he brooded over them. In reply to a letter from Georg Erdmann, an old schoolfriend, once his companion in the choir at Lüneburg and now Russian diplomatic and commercial agent in Danzig, he had responded detailing his woes in graphic fashion. But Erdmann had written in 1726, and it took Bach no less than four years to reply. The fact that he finally troubled to do so in October 1730 – in other words, *after* Gesner's more congenial rectorship had begun – suggests that the wounds of his Leipzig quarrels went deep. His letter was one way of explaining the situation to himself.

> Honoured Sir,
> Pray excuse an old and faithful servant troubling you with this letter. It is nearly four years since you were good enough to answer the last I wrote to you, when you were pleased to desire news of me and my welfare. I will do my best to comply with your wish. You know my *fata* up to the *mutation* which took me to Cöthen as Capellmeister. Its gracious Prince loved and understood music, so that I expected to end my days there. But my *Serenissimus* married a Bernburg wife, and in consequence, so it seemed, his musical inclination abated, while his new Princess proved to be an *amusa*. So it pleased God to call me here as Director Musices and Cantor of the Thomasschule. At first I found it not altogether agreeable to become a simple Cantor after having been a Capellmeister, and for that reason I forebore from coming to a *resolution* for three months. However, I received such favourable reports of the *situation*, that, having particularly in my mind my sons' *studia*, and after invoking divine guidance, I at last made up my mind, came to Leipzig, performed my *Probe*, and received the post. And here, God willing, I have remained till now. But unfortunately I have discovered that (1) this situation is not as good as it was represented to be, (2) various *accidentia* relative to my *station* have been withdrawn, (3) living is expensive, and (4) my masters are strange folk with very little care for music in them. Consequently, I am subjected to constant annoyance,

jealousy, and persecution. It is therefore in my mind, with God's assistance, to seek my *fortune* elsewhere. If your Honour knows of or should hear of a *convenable station* in your town, I beg you to let me have your valuable *recommendation*. Nothing will be wanting on my part to give *satisfaction*, show diligence, and justify your much esteemed support. My present *station* is worth about 700 thalers a year, and if the death-rate is higher than *ordinairement* my *accidentia* increase in *proportion*; but Leipzig is a healthy place, and for the past year, as it happens, I have received about 100 kronen less than usual in funeral *accidentia*. The cost of living, too, is so *excessive* that I was better off in Thuringia on 400 thalers.

And now I must tell you something of my domestic circumstances. My first wife died at Cöthen and I have married again. Of my first marriage are living three sons and a daughter, whom your Honour saw at Weimar and may be pleased to remember. Of my second marriage one son and two daughters are living. My eldest son is a *studiosus juris*, the other two are at school here in the *prima* and *secunda classis*; my eldest daughter as yet is unmarried. My children by my second wife are still young; the eldest boy is six. All my children are born *musici*; from my own *familie*, I assure you, I can arrange a concert *vocaliter* and *instrumentaliter*; my wife, in particular, has a very clear soprano, and my eldest daughter can give a good account of herself too. I should trespass too far on your forbearance were I to *incommode* your Honour further. I conclude therefore with my most devoted and lifelong *respect*.

As we have seen, Gesner's reforms and his personal influence went a long way towards calming Bach's doubts, but Gesner's reign at St Thomas's was short-lived. An able and ambitious man, he had no more desire than Bach to remain a mere schoolmaster, and in 1734 he was called to a university professorship at the new university of Göttingen, where he was to have a long and distinguished career. Gesner was succeeded as Rector by Johann August Ernesti (no relation to the previous Ernesti), Conrector of the Thomasschule since Pezold's death in 1731. Like his predecessor, Ernesti was a classical scholar and philologist. A young man who wished to continue and deepen Gesner's improvements – he was only twenty-seven when appointed Rector – Ernesti was altogether more radical in his approach to reform. Though himself a theological scholar of some distinction, in educational matters he was a rationalist who shared the increasingly secular outlook of his generation. A school's purpose in their eyes was to fit its pupils for the world, not for heaven; for practical life, not for speculation. At the same time, they deplored what would now be called vocational training: the acquisition of useful skills. The role of a great school was to teach boys how to become scholars, administrators, lawyers, men of affairs, leaders of their professions.

Ernesti's determination to bring the school up to date, and his laudable ambition to raise academic standards, entailed major changes in the curriculum. Such changes were being made in schools throughout Europe, and they were to shape secondary education throughout the eighteenth and nineteenth centuries as religious foundations were secularized. In particular, music and theology – hitherto the central subjects in the Thomasschule curriculum – were deeply affected. Though the teaching of religion remained the basis of all education, the philosophical and metaphysical aspects of theology gave way to scripture history and church doctrine, learnt mainly by rote. The kind of subtle theological debate which so delighted Bach was now confined to professional divines.

The emphasis on pragmatism, combined with a distaste for vocational skills, meant that music was doubly damned in Ernesti's view. On the one hand, it smelt of the medieval curriculum, rank with useless theory and mystical numerology. On the other, it was a matter of mere technical competence. Neither way was it likely to lead to an important or useful career. When, after many years as Rector, he drew up new regulations for what was, after all, a choir school, music was not even mentioned. Gesner had spoken of boys dedicating their musical talents to God's service and finding themselves thereby in touch with divine harmony. It is reported that when Ernesti came upon boys practising their instruments he would say disdainfully 'So, you mean to be a pot-house fiddler'.

But theology and music – and more especially the relationship between them – were not only the core of the old Thomasschule curriculum: they were the very foundation of Bach's life and work. The combination was almost certainly one of the things which had drawn him away from congenial Cöthen to Leipzig. However desirable Ernesti's reforms might be for the school, therefore, to Bach they could only represent an undermining of his very being. How far he was conscious of this as such we cannot say. More likely, he experienced it as an intensification of his practical difficulties with the authorities. What we can say is that within a very short time of the new Rector's arrival, the two men were engaged in a furious quarrel which made Bach's previous clashes with the university and the council look very minor indeed.

To begin with, Rector and Cantor got on well. Bach wrote a cantata for Ernesti's installation in November 1734, and the Rector stood as godfather to Bach's last two sons. Then things began to go wrong. A series of small mishaps and misunderstandings involving Bach's authority over the boys culminated in a public row when the Cantor's choir prefect, Gottfried Theodor Krause, punished some pupils for misbehaving at a wedding. According to Krause's own account, he had been specifically charged by the Cantor to supervise the choristers, with authority to punish them as he thought fit, if necessary. He had first admonished the unruly boys and only then, when they continued to misbehave, administered the cane. One of the boys alleged that the punishment was severe enough to lacerate his back. Though the school hairdresser, doubling as medical attendant, could find no sign of injury, the indignant victim took his complaint to Ernesti, and the Rector, deeming the punishment too severe, ordered Krause to be flogged in public – itself an unusually harsh punishment, not least because Krause was no child but a young man of twenty-two. Supported by Bach, Krause appealed against the punishment – an appeal the Rector ignored. He then asked to be allowed to leave the school, and again the Rector refused. Deciding not to wait for the flogging, Krause absconded and the Rector appointed another Krause (unrelated to the first) in his place.

The affair infuriated Bach on five counts: first because Krause One was his own candidate as prefect, second because the Rector ignored his plea to spare the youth, third because Krause Two (as Bach and Ernesti had earlier agreed) was a dubious character with loose morals and little musical skill, and fourth because it was the Cantor's right to choose the prefects, not the Rector's. But the fifth reason for his anger was the most important. The proposed flogging of Krause One and the appointment of Krause Two were public rebukes to Bach himself. It was quite clearly the Cantor's duty to supervise the choirboys at weddings. However, it was also clear that, though he might deputize the power of supervision to Krause, he was *not* authorized by school statutes to invest the prefect with the right to administer punishment. In short, by sending a prefect in his place, and then by allowing him to exceed his rights, Bach could be said to have caused the trouble in the first place. The Cantor had been derelict in his duty. He had also encroached on the Rector's powers. By insisting on the flogging of Krause One, Ernesti was underlining both failings.

Bach responded by asserting his own right to appoint the choir prefects. As the row developed, he argued his case in two letters to the council written in August 1736. The Rector meanwhile replied, accusing Bach of misrepresenting the facts and hinting that the Cantor was open to bribery. But the quarrel was not confined to an exchange of letters. While the councillors wondered what to do, Bach took action, expelling Krause Two from the choir-loft on successive Sundays and replacing him with another prefect who was sent to apprise the Rector of his appointment. Bach, it is said, chased away Krause Two 'with great shouting and noise' whereupon the Rector sent him back, threatening the choir with retribution if they flouted his will.

The dispute dragged on throughout the second half of 1736 and it was not until February 1737 that the council decided to act, postponing the announcement of their decision for a further two months. Both participants were reproved, Ernesti for his clumsy handling of the affair, Bach for failure to attend the wedding which had caused the original problem. Krause Two being due to leave the school at Easter 1737, the councillors hoped that the whole affair would die a natural death. But Bach was not satisfied with this judgment and in August 1737 he petitioned the consistory. This body had already considered the matter and referred it to the council, and Bach may well have been counting on the rivalry between the two authorities to enlist the consistory on his side. His petition shows just how far he was prepared to go. It argues that the school regulations of 1723 governing, among other things, the appointment of prefects, had never been ratified, and that the case should therefore have been judged according to the old regulations – which were, of course, more favourable to Bach. The consistory took no action itself but forwarded the letter to the council who hoped once again that the matter would die down and decided to do nothing about it. But Bach had the bit between his teeth and in October 1737 he took his case to the elector at Dresden.

On the face of it, this was a very canny move. Twelve months before, he had finally achieved a long-standing ambition with appointment to the elector's Kapelle as *Hofcompositeur.* As a court official he could naturally expect a degree of royal protection. In December, the elector duly ordered the consistory to examine the matter once more. Taking note of this request in February the following year, the consistory asked for a further report from the council!

It is not known how – or even whether – this bureaucratic farce ended, though Spitta suggests that the elector may have intervened personally when he visited Leipzig in 1738 and Bach's collegium musicum performed in front of his house once more. But a chronicler writing much later in the eighteenth century noted that the affair reverberated far beyond the personal relations of Bach and Ernesti: 'Since that time there has been little harmony between the Rector and the Cantor, although both posts have changed hands several times.' No doubt this exaggerates the significance of a single quarrel which was more symptom than cause. For what the tensions between Bach and Ernesti reveal is that the days of the old-fashioned choir school were numbered, even in conservative Leipzig. Ernesti's determination to enforce his authority, at whatever cost, is a sign that the world Bach had grown up in was coming to an end. This is surely the real reason why trivial events awoke such deep, passionate and lasting bitterness.

Having annoyed the council, the university and the church, Bach had thus completed his good work by alienating the school authorities. Who can say how much this contributed towards his increasing retreat into a private creative world – or, on the other hand, how much the need for that retreat prompted his many quarrels? Whatever the causes, from the mid-1730s to the end of his life, Bach turned more and more to pure musical forms. After a career of thirty years attending to the demands of practical music-making, he was now able and inclined to devote himself to an almost mystical fulfilment of his art in the quintessence of counterpoint as celestial arithmetic.

Paradoxically, this esoteric tendency is strikingly evident in one of his most accessible later works. The patent of Bach's appointment as Hofcompositeur was conveyed to him by Count Carl von Keyserlingk, Russian envoy at Dresden. The count was a music lover who had attended at least one of the organ recitals Bach gave in Dresden after his appointment. As a victim of chronic insomnia, he employed one Johann Gottlieb Goldberg to play the clavier to him, so that he might be soothed and distracted on sleepless nights. Goldberg was a pupil of Bach's in 1741, and so it came about (according to Forkel) that the count commissioned from the new Hofcompositeur a set of clavier variations for harpsichord with two manuals or keyboards. As payment, Bach was presented by the count with a golden goblet filled with golden coins, and the work has been known ever since as the 'Goldberg' Variations.

Despite Forkel's testimony, this charming story does not quite add up. The *Aria mit verschiedenen Veränderungen* or 'Aria with divers Variations' – to give the piece its proper title – was published in 1742 when Goldberg was fifteen, and probably written earlier: the Aria is taken from one of Bach's notebooks dating from 1725. Even in that age of sweated labour, it seems hardly likely that Count Keyserlingk would have kept a child up all night for his own diversion. More probably, the work acquired its association after publication. But the circumstances of composition hardly matter. What counts is that the Goldberg Variations combine intellectual sophistication with great beauty. No knowledge of their daunting contrapuntal intricacy is needed to enjoy them – though, of course, such knowledge can greatly enhance one's enjoyment.

In later life, Bach became increasingly preoccupied with the science of numbers and his preoccupation is omnipresent in this work, as in other pieces written or assembled at the time, such as the chorale preludes gathered in *Clavier-Übung* III, published in 1739. Western numerology is derived largely from the Bible. There being three persons in the Trinity, for example – the Father, the Son and the Holy Ghost – much of Bach's music is shaped by the number three. *Clavier-Übung* III is dominated by three and its multiples: fugues with three subjects, groups of nine and six pieces – twenty-seven pieces in all. In the Goldberg Variations there are thirty variations divided into groups of three. Every third variation, except for the last, is a canon. There are therefore nine canons altogether, i.e. three times three. All the canons are in two voices with an independent bass, making three voices in each. Each canon is at a different interval, with the voices gradually spreading apart, so the first canon is at the unison, the last at the ninth. The last variation of all *sounds* like a canon with its imitative entries. It is in fact a quodlibet of the sort Bach and his relations used to sing at their jolly family gatherings: a mixture of popular tunes – including *Kraut und Rüben haben mich vertrieben* ('cabbage and turnips have driven me away') – over a statement of the bass line from the original theme. Finally, that theme returns to complete the work – or to begin it again, a possibility which suggests that the entire set of variations is like a giant round which could go on endlessly.

*   *   *

It hardly needs saying that not all Bach's time at Leipzig was taken up with niggling professional quarrels or with work. His family continued to expand until 1742 with the birth of his twentieth and last child, Regina Susanna. Among these late children, Johann Christoph Friedrich, born in 1732, and Johann Christian, three years his junior, were to join the other outstanding musical members of the Bach family. It is pleasant to think that, amidst all his trials, Johann Sebastian survived long enough to see their talents, too, beginning to flower.

He also continued to follow the blossoming careers of his elder children with close attention. But despite the success of Wilhelm Friedemann and Carl Philipp Emanuel and the delight of siring new children in his fifties, all was not well with Bach. In family matters as in professional life, his fortunes took a downward turn in the mid 1730s. One of his sons, Gottfried

Heinrich, though musically gifted, proved to be feeble-minded. Another caused him great heartache, not least because the boy's considerable talents went to waste and he died just as he seemed to be recovering from early troubles.

In 1735, Johann Gottfried Bernhard, Bach's third surviving son, then aged twenty, was appointed organist at St Mary's Church in Mühlhausen. Though his father's influence with the mayor obviously helped, the boy gave an excellent audition and could certainly have achieved professional success on his merits. But Johann Gottfried found no more luck in Mühlhausen than his father had, nearly thirty years earlier. Several councillors who favoured another candidate remained hostile and the council minutes record their all too familiar complaints. According to one, Gottfried

Bach's youngest son, Johann Christian, painted in London by Thomas Gainsborough.

Bernhard Bach had 'preluded far too much and too long, and thus unduly shortened the time meant for the service and the devotion', while another claimed: 'If Bach continues to play in this way, the organ will be ruined in two years or most of the congregation will be deaf.'

When Johann Gottfried left Mühlhausen in March 1737, the local candidate succeeded to the job, and Bach's son moved on to Sangerhausen where his father's personal and family influence again smoothed the way. On this occasion Johann Sebastian wrote to an old friend, Johann Friedrich Klemm, who was a member of the Sangerhausen council, recalling his own connection with the town:

> So, in God's good providence, it may come about that you will be able to fulfil on behalf of a son of mine the good will you showed to my unworthy self some thirty years ago, when, too, the post of figural organist was vacant.

Under the presidency of the late Burgermeister Vollrath, I then obtained
the vote, though the higher powers advanced another candidate, and for
that *raison* I had to abandon my good fortune. Your Honour will not take
it amiss that I refer to my *fata* on that occasion, for my *entrée* in this present
correspondence has received so gracious an *ingress* that I am fain to see the
finger of God's providence in it.

In April 1737 Johann Gottfried was duly appointed to the post, but he
had left unpaid bills at Mühlhausen and ran up more at Sangerhausen,
and the end of it all was that, after little more than a year, he disappeared
from the town leaving behind him only his chattels and debts. Once
again his father stepped in, and another of Bach's few extant letters is an
embarrassed and even anguished plea for patience, dated 24 May 1738,
and addressed once again to Herr Klemm:

You will not take it amiss that I have not till now answered your esteemed
letter, for I only returned from Dresden two days ago. So loving and tender
a father as yourself will understand the grief and sorrow with which I write
this letter. I have not seen my, alas, undutiful boy since last year, when I
enjoyed so many kindnesses at your hands. Your Honour will remember
that I then paid what he owed for his board at Mühlhausen, discharged the
bond which seems to have been the cause of his leaving that place, and left
a sum of money to meet his other debts, hoping that for the future he
would reform his *genus vitae*. You will therefore understand how pained and
surprised I am to learn that he has again been borrowing money on all
sides, has not in the least changed his *genus vitae*, and has absconded without
giving me, so far, the slightest indication of his whereabouts. What can I
do or say more, my warnings having failed, and my loving care and help
having proved unavailing? I can only bear my cross in patience and
commend my undutiful boy to God's mercy, never doubting that He will
hear my sorrow-stricken prayer and in His good time bring my son to
understand that the path of conversion leads to Him.

Here we find Bach turning very characteristically between grief, hope
and resignation to God's will, a sequence of feelings so familiar from his
cantatas. But hope was to be frustrated and the story has an unhappy
ending, for just a year from the date of Bach's letter to Klemm, and four
months after registering in the law faculty at the university of Jena,

Johann Gottfried succumbed to a fever and died in 1739, aged twenty-four.

While Johann Gottfried's troubles were brewing up at Sangerhausen, his second cousin, Johann Elias Bach, arrived from Schweinfurt (where his father was Cantor) to study divinity in Leipzig. By this time, Bach's three elder sons had all left home. Wilhelm Friedemann was still organist at St Sophia's church in Dresden where he remained until he moved to Halle in 1746. After a spell at Leipzig University, Carl Philipp Emanuel had transferred his studies to Frankfurt an der Oder. In 1738 he went to Berlin where he was appointed court accompanist to King Frederick II in 1740. These young men had been Bach's pupils and companions. Apart from one spinster daughter, all the other children living at home were in their teens or younger. So it was natural for a man who enjoyed the company of the young, and cultivated strong family piety, to invite Johann Elias to join his household.

At the age of thirty-three Johann Elias had decided to resume university studies earlier cut short by poverty. Now, with a scholarship from his native town and help from a rich patron, he joined the Leipzig theological faculty. In return for board and lodging, he was invited to act as Johann Sebastian's secretary and help teach his three younger sons. A formal contract of employment was signed and he remained in Bach's house from 1738 to 1742. He was a most amiable man with great respect and admiration for his kinsman and especially for Anna Magdalena. It is from Johann Elias' letters, many of which have been preserved, that we get our best portrait of Bach's second wife. Clearly a warm-hearted and attractive woman, she was capable of inspiring love and devotion. Johann Elias refers to her in correspondence as 'Frau Muhme' – an untranslatable term which means literally 'Mrs Aunt', but has strong overtones of affection. Writing to his mother in 1738, he mentions that

> I should like to give some yellow carnations to our Frau Muhme; she loves the garden and would be so pleased to have them …

In another letter he says she is waiting for the flowers with all the excitement of a child before Christmas; when they arrive she tends them 'as carefully as a child, lest harm befall them'. She was also fond of singing birds. In poor health for many years before her death, and often confined to the house, she took her pleasures where she could find them. She suffered a serious illness in 1741, though she survived to give birth to her last child in the following year.

Her husband, on the other hand, continued to live a very active life, making frequent trips away from Leipzig, though work and pleasure now provided equal motives, and he took the opportunity whenever he could to visit Wilhelm Friedemann in Dresden and Carl Philipp Emanuel in Berlin. During the last decade of his life the quarrels of his middle years appear to have become a thing of the past, if only because he now ignored the Leipzig authorities and went his own way. He wrote little new music for the Thomasschule choir and even his normal musical duties were largely performed by a deputy appointed in 1740. When taxed with failings by council or consistory he replied with indifference rather than passion.

Though he neglected his school duties, Bach continued to take pupils of his own – always provided, as C. P. E. Bach told Forkel, they showed talent and application to their work. Several were Leipzig University students, including Johann Christoph Altnikol, a member of Bach's collegium musicum. After graduating from the university, Altnikol continued to work with Bach who helped him to secure the post of organist at a church in Naumberg in 1748. In the January following, Altnikol married Bach's second surviving daughter, Elisabeth. According to Forkel he attended the composer in his final days, taking down music from dictation, including the chorale prelude *Vor deinen Thron tret' ich* (BWV668) which is believed to be Bach's last composition.

Despite his increasing detachment from institutional life in Leipzig, Bach was by no means free from controversies in his final years. The most serious was inaugurated by an article published in May 1737 which attacked not only his music but the aesthetic behind it. The piece appeared anonymously, but it soon became known that the writer was Johann Adolf Scheibe who had recently begun issuing in Hamburg a new musical journal, *Der critische Musikus*. Like many new journals, *Der critische Musikus* tried to establish itself by championing the new and ridiculing the old. Scheibe, who later became court conductor to Christian VI of Denmark, was the son of a distinguished organ builder. Old Scheibe's work was well-known to Bach, who inspected and praised at least three of his organs. Young Scheibe had himself been an unsuccessful candidate for the post of organist at the Leipzig Nikolaikirche in 1729 when Bach was an examiner. It is sometimes claimed that he took against Bach because of his failure at Leipzig. He certainly seems to have made ill-natured comments about the judges, Bach included. If small-minded, this would hardly be surprising. Philipp Spitta (Bach's great nineteenth-century biographer) goes further and suggests that Bach responded by lampooning Scheibe in the doggerel verse of his cantata *Phoebus and Pan*, as King Midas the ass:

> Empty heads and swollen, lacking wit and gumption,
> Rightly feel the fool's cap sticking on their crown.
> He who's never seen a ship,
> Takes the rudder in his grip,
> And saileth the ocean inexpert, will drown!

Spitta's enjoyable speculation is undermined a little by the fact that Bach wrote a friendly testimonial for Scheibe two years after he failed in Leipzig.

Nor is there necessarily any personal animus behind Scheibe's criticism of Bach's music. Two years later, in 1739, he went out of his way to praise the Italian Concerto, perhaps because it conformed with his view that music 'must naturally be pleasant and tickle the ear'. When he attacked Bach, Scheibe was voicing a common opinion at the time that the composer, though brilliant and profoundly gifted, was wasting his gifts on over-elaborate music in an outdated style. In line with the growing contemporary taste for naturalness and expressiveness in art, he found in much of Bach's music only wearisome artifice. After conceding his victim's supremacy as a keyboard player (perhaps to ensure that no one suspected him of pique), Scheibe complains that

> This great man would be the wonder of the universe if his compositions displayed more agreeable qualities, were less turgid and sophisticated, more

simple and natural in character. His music is exceedingly difficult to play, because the efficiency of his own limbs sets his standards; he expects singers and players to be as agile with voice and instrument as he is with his fingers, which is impossible. Grace-notes and embellishments, such as a player instinctively supplies, he puts down in actual symbols, a habit which not only sacrifices the harmonic beauty of his music but also blurs its melodic line. All his parts, too, are equally melodic, so that one cannot distinguish the principal tune among them. In short he is as a musician what Herr von Lohenstein used to be as a poet: pomposity diverts them both from a natural to an artificial style, changing what might have been sublime into the obscure. In regard to both of them, we wonder at an effort so laboured and, since nothing comes of it, so futile.

Friends and admirers soon sprang to Bach's defence. In January 1738, Johann Abraham Birnbaum, a lecturer in rhetoric at Leipzig University, published a six-page pamphlet in which he took particular exception to Scheibe's description of his subject as a mere *Musikant* – an ordinary musician – when Bach was so clearly 'ein grosser Componist, ein *Meister* der Music' – a great composer, a *master* of music.

But when Scheibe says that 'All his parts, too, are equally melodic, so that one cannot distinguish the principal tune among them', it has to be admitted that he identifies (however crudely) a problem which many listeners still have with Bach's late works, however familiar they may be with his earlier music. It is unlikely that any music lover has difficulty with the Brandenburg Concertos, for example, although the counterpoint is often complex, because the brilliance of the instrumentation leads the ear to dominant voices, in the process making the structures of these works crystal clear. But in the great compositions of Bach's last years – the Goldberg Variations, the second book of the *Well-tempered Clavier*, the chorale preludes collected in *Clavier-Übung* III, the Canonic Variations on *Vom Himmel hoch*, the *Musical Offering*, the volume of eighteen chorale preludes on which he was working at the time of his death, and above all in his crowning masterpiece, the *Art of Fugue* – the instrumental medium becomes progressively less important, the form and contrapuntal texture everything. It is as though Scheibe were not describing Bach's past in 1737 so much as predicting his future.

The point is worth emphasizing because, as we saw from Bach's 1730 memorandum to the Leipzig town council, he was as well aware as anyone of changing fashions in music. Indeed, many of his own works reflect those fashions. The delightful small pieces he composed and adapted in the Notebooks he produced for Anna Magdalena and Wilhelm Friedemann, for example, are often in the fashionable *style galant* which was to influence the work of his own sons, who in turn influenced Mozart. Bach was exceptionally sensitive to nuances of musical style. The effect of his studies in French and Italian music is clear enough evidence of that. One could argue that the Brandenburg Concertos and the Italian Concerto are more brilliant 'Italian' music than anything ever written inside Italy.

But the crucial argument against Scheibe still needs putting. Bach was never an 'artificial' composer in the bad sense of that word. He never wrote paper music, pleasing to the eye but not to the ear. Sound is always his primary concern. And just because Scheibe and others like him were frightened by the complexity of Bach's music, there is no reason why we should follow them. Even at his most dauntingly theoretical, as in the *Art of Fugue*, Bach balances technical ingenuity and philosophical interest with practicality and beauty. We have seen how this combination

The music room at Potsdam (destroyed in 1945) with a Silbermann piano. Bach probably played here when he visited Frederick the Great in 1747.

works in the Goldberg Variations, but there is no more dazzling example of it than the *Musical Offering*, the piece occasioned by the last great journey of Bach's career, his visit to the king of Prussia in 1747.

C. P. E. Bach had married in 1744 and Johann Sebastian had not yet seen his first grandchild, Johann August. When he visited Potsdam, near Berlin, with Wilhelm Friedemann in the spring of 1747, his daughter-in-law was again pregnant. Carl Philipp Emanuel was then in the service of Frederick the Great, who adored music: whenever the opera house was closed, dinner in the palace was always preceded by a concert with music chosen by the king, who liked to distribute the orchestral parts with his own hand. Bach was therefore bound to be invited to the palace, and the summons was considered important enough to merit official report in the Berlin newspaper. Years later, Wilhelm Friedemann gave a more colourful account of the occasion to Forkel:

> At this time the King had every evening a private Concert, in which he himself generally performed some Concertos on the flute. One evening, just as he was getting his flute ready, and his musicians were assembled, an officer brought with him a list of the strangers who had arrived. With his flute in his hand he ran over the list, but immediately turned to the assembled musicians, and said with a kind of agitation, 'Gentlemen, old Bach is come.' The flute was now laid aside; and old Bach, who had alighted at his son's lodgings, was immediately summoned to the palace ...
>
> The King gave up his Concert for this evening, and invited Bach, then already called the Old Bach, to try his fortepianos, made by Silbermann, which stood in several rooms of the palace. The musicians went with him from room to room, and Bach was invited everywhere to try and to play unpremeditated compositions. After he had gone on for some time, he asked the King to give him a subject for a Fugue, in order to execute it immediately without any preparation. The King admired the learned manner in which his subject was thus executed extempore; and, probably to see how far such art could be carried, expressed a wish to hear a Fugue with six Obbligato Parts. But as it is not every subject that is fit for such full harmony, Bach chose one himself, and immediately executed it to the astonishment of all present in the same magnificent and learned manner as he had done that of the King. His Majesty desired also to hear his performance on the organ. The next day therefore Bach was taken to all

the organs in Potsdam, as he had before been to Silbermann's fortepianos. After his return to Leipsig, he composed the subject, which he had received from the King, in three and six parts, added several artificial passages in strict canon to it, and had it engraved, under the title of 'Musicalisches Opfer' (Musical Offering), and dedicated it to the inventor.

Though some of the details of Wilhelm Friedemann's account conflict with other reports of this encounter, the substance of what he told Forkel is certainly true. When Bach returned to Leipzig after his triumphant journey to Berlin, he composed the *Musical Offering*, a series of pieces including a flute sonata (in compliment to the flautist king) and an intricate reworking of the royal subject in a magnificent six-part fugue. One hundred copies were printed, and Bach gave some away and sold others at one thaler each. Frederick was sent a specially bound and printed presentation copy with a fulsome dedication. It is not known whether the composer received anything in return.

In the same year as the *Musical Offering*, 1747, he joined a society founded by one of his former pupils in Leipzig. While a theological student at the university, Lorenz Christoph Mizler had been a member of Bach's collegium musicum. In 1734 he wrote a thesis, 'On whether the art of music is part of philosophic knowledge', which he dedicated to the composer. As the title of this thesis suggests, Mizler was intrigued by the search for the mathematical foundations of music and its harmonic

This romantic picture (1852) by Adolph von Menzel of Frederick the Great playing the flute, shows C. P. E. Bach at the harpsichord.

and contrapuntal first principles. Just as Isaac Newton had recently revealed the fundamental laws of gravitation and attraction, so, Mizler believed, could the laws of sound be established. In 1736 he founded a periodical, the *Musicalische Bibliothek*, devoted to this end, and in 1738 this periodical became the house journal of a new Societät der Musicalischen Wissenschaften – Society for the Promotion of Musical Knowledge ('Wissenschaften' can also mean science or wisdom).

Mizler was not alone in his quest. Nor is it quite as aridly theoretical as it sounds. In the same period, the French composer Jean-Philippe Rameau published several volumes expounding his scientific theory of harmony – a theory which he exemplified in his own music. And there was a common belief in the early eighteenth century, inspired by the work of Newton and Locke, Descartes and Leibniz, that all human knowledge could be explained scientifically – just as medieval philosophers had thought that all knowledge could be explained in theological terms. This belief applied to music and poetry as much as to chemistry or physics.

The original edition of Bach's Canon BWV1076.

Among the early members of Mizler's society were Handel, Telemann and Carl Heinrich Graun, Frederick the Great's Kapellmeister. Bach was elected to membership in 1747. Each member was required by the rules to make an annual contribution to society archives in the form of a musical work or a treatise on musical theory. The members were also expected to present the society library with portraits. Bach was therefore painted by the Dresden court painter, Elias Gottlob Haussmann, and the portrait still survives. It shows him holding the triple six-part Canon (BWV1076) he wrote as his first offering. This was published in the *Musicalische Bibliothek* four years after Bach's death, in 1754. It is probable that the Canonic Variations on *Vom Himmel hoch* were also written for Mizler's society.

Although they expressed themselves in very different terms, the new scientific thinkers had one thing in common with the old theologians: a belief in the vital importance of numbers. Newton and Leibniz, for example, both invented forms of differential calculus, the mathematical system which made the new physics of motion possible. And Newton, who was a profoundly religious man, believed that in exploring the mathematical relationships which govern matter, he was uncovering the laws of nature and thereby revealing the divine harmony of the universe. In this context, Bach's interest in numerology is not the narrowly backward-looking obsession it can seem, but one form of a deep-seated need which has preoccupied human beings from the earliest times to the present: the need to make logical and harmonious sense from the diverse phenomena of existence by revealing its underlying laws. Music has always seemed to philosophers from Pythagoras onwards to be an appealing way of doing this because, by expressing abstract truths in concrete terms, it can lead the soul to the apprehension of eternal wisdom through its perception of earthly beauty.

And that is the context in which we need to consider two masterpieces of Bach's last years: the final version of the Mass in B minor, and *Die Kunst der Fuge* – 'The Art of Fugue' – which some scholars believe was meant as a contribution to Mizler's society. Both works are problematic when considered as single units, and it is not clear how or even whether Bach envisaged performances. The enormous Mass was assembled over many years, most of the movements recycle earlier cantatas, and the style changes abruptly from section to section, ranging from archaic fugues to fashionable Italianate ritornellos. If the Mass can seem bewilderingly diverse, the intensity and unity of purpose in the *Art of Fugue* present audiences with exactly the opposite problem. Here is a work whose relentless explorations of the contrapuntal possibilities in a single theme make the greatest intellectual demands. This work grew directly out of the *Musical Offering*, which is also an extended development of one motif. The themes are similar, and the music he wrote for the king of Prussia clearly stimulated Bach's urge to stretch his technique to the limits by composing his basic idea into every imaginable polyphonic combination. As with the Goldberg Variations and the *Well-tempered Clavier*, the *Art of Fugue* was meant to fulfil several functions at once, being a demonstration of the composer's skill, a manual of contrapuntal devices and a test for performers. But in this case the work also represents the consummation of a whole career. That would be so, even if Bach had lived to compose more music, instead of dying before he could finish the score, though he had already begun to engrave it. As if to signal its personal importance to him, the composer worked his own name into the music. In German musical notation B stands for B flat and H for B natural, thus spelling out the theme B♭—A—C—B♮. When Carl Philipp Emanuel published the work in 1751, he noted on the manuscript at the point where the music stops, that 'While working on this fugue, where the name BACH is introduced as a countersubject, the author died.'

The last page of the Art of Fugue *in Bach's autograph, with a note by C. P. E. Bach recording the place where his father broke off.*

Although C. P. E. Bach claimed in his father's Obituary that Bach remained in good heart up to the last weeks of his life, his health seems to have deteriorated throughout 1749. He can hardly have been encouraged to recover by the fact that news of his illness provoked blatant lobbying for the succession to his post at the Thomasschule. The elector of Saxony's chief minister, Count Heinrich von Brühl, wrote to Leipzig Burgomeister Born in June 1749 to recommend his own candidate, Gottlob Harrer. The councillors, no doubt placed in an awkward position by pressure from the powerful von Brühl, neatly side-stepped the embarrassment. They responded by inviting Harrer to audition, which he did with great success, but declined to proceed any further for the time being. Though it was not unusual to consider candidates for the succession to such a post in the lifetime of the incumbent, it cannot have been pleasant for Bach.

His eyesight, weak by nature and strained by years of intensive work in poor light, also worsened. On the advice of friends, he decided to consult a specialist, the English 'ophthalmiater' (as he called himself) John Taylor, who was on an extensive tour of Germany, treating distinguished patients. In his *History* published years later, Taylor seems to recall Bach in jumbled fashion when he remarks that

> I have seen a vast variety of singular animals, such as dromedaries, camels, etc., and particularly at Leipsic, where a celebrated master of music, who had already arrived to his 88th year, received his sight by my hands; it is with this very man that the famous Handel was first educated, and with whom I once thought to have had the same success, having all circumstances in his favour, motions of the pupil, light etc., but, upon drawing the curtain, we found the bottom defective from a paralytic disorder.

Taylor operated on Bach twice in the spring of 1750, but despite his initial success, the treatment failed and the composer was left with partial sight at best. He also seems to have experienced either a mild stroke or post-operative trauma, his constitution perhaps weakened by drugs. Making a partial recovery, he continued to work, instructing pupils and composing pieces for a new collection of eighteen chorale preludes, completing seventeen in his own handwriting, but his health was shattered and he declined rapidly in May and June. Bach's daughter Elisabeth and her husband, Altnikol, were summoned, and Altnikol began to take down from Bach's dictation the final chorale prelude, the reworking of an earlier piece. It breaks off in the twenty-sixth bar.

As the words of the chorale to which this music was adapted make clear, Bach's thoughts were firmly fixed on death:

> Before thy throne my God, I stand,
> Myself, my all, are in Thy hand;
> Turn to me Thine approving face,
> Nor from me now withhold Thy grace.
>
> Grant that my end may worthy be,
> And that I wake Thy face to see,
> Thyself for evermore to know!
> Amen, amen, God grant it so.

On 18 July his health suddenly improved and his sight was restored, but the improvement was temporary. The composer rapidly succumbed to a stroke and then a burning fever, and died at a quarter to nine on Tuesday evening, 28 July 1750.

Bach was buried three days later in the graveyard of the Johanniskirche, but the whereabouts of his grave was soon forgotten. Only in 1950 were his remains transferred to the Thomaskirche. Because he left no will, Bach's property was divided between his widow and his nine surviving children. Anna Magdalena received one third of an estate valued at 1,159 thalers 16 groschen, less 153 thalers of debts and expenses. Her total inheritance amounted to 335 thalers – about half of Bach's annual income – on which she had to support herself, two daughters and an unmarried stepdaughter. It is hardly surprising that she died in an almshouse ten years later.

An inventory of Bach's possessions made after his death includes a small library, nineteen musical instruments, cash, household goods, silver and other items, but none of his music. Apart from a few cantatas presented to the Thomasschule by Anna Magdalena, his manuscripts were divided between the two eldest sons. Carl Philipp Emanuel's share of this incomparable patrimony eventually reached the Royal Library in Berlin, but in 1774 poverty forced Wilhelm Friedemann to auction most of the scores remaining in his possession.

On 7 August 1750, just over a week after the composer's death, the council met to elect a new Cantor. Bach's name was hardly mentioned, except by one councillor who reiterated a familiar cry with evident feeling: 'The school needs a Cantor, not a Kapellmeister.' Count von Brühl's candidate, Gottlob Harrer, was duly elected, and the good burghers of Leipzig consigned his troublesome predecessor to oblivion.

CHAPTER 8

Solo Instrumental Music

Although Bach was for most of his professional life primarily engaged in composing and performing music for the church, his secular works have proved a good deal more popular in modern times. This reflects a change in social and musical conditions, but it may also have something to do with the fact that we encounter the composer most intimately in the solo instrumental works, especially in the cello suites, the violin partitas and the *Well-tempered Clavier*. But there is one place where all the aspects of Bach's life, personal and professional, public and private, secular and religious, come together – a place where every aspect of his musical personality is revealed – namely, in the organ music. Bach left over 250 pieces for the instrument, and certainly wrote many more, most of them composed for himself or his pupils to play. The organ was like a lifelong friend, thoroughly known and loved, with whom all his thoughts could be shared. Significantly, his final work, written when he probably knew he was dying, was a set of organ chorale preludes. The last fragment from this set concludes our selection of music.

Bach's organ works are traditionally divided into two groups: those based on chorales (mainly the chorale preludes and early *Partite diverse*), and the so-called 'free' compositions, including preludes, fantasias, toccatas, transcriptions and fugues. Among the three pieces we have chosen, there is a late chorale prelude and an early free composition. But as the third, middle-period work shows, the distinction is by no means watertight. The Passacaglia in C minor is not based on a chorale, but it *is* founded on a recurring bass theme which governs the work in the same manner. This passacaglia is typical of the way Bach continued to experiment formally throughout his composing life: many of the later chorale preludes are very freely composed, while there are 'free' pieces based on chorale melodies or plainsong chant. This reminds us that what matters more than the distinction between free and chorale-based pieces is the shaping

A Renaissance organ, engraved in 1620.

of the entire oeuvre by an abiding and increasingly subtle preoccupation with counterpoint.

Counterpoint is in essence the sounding of distinct melodic lines at the same time. The dominant contrapuntal forms are canon and fugue. Canon is the strictest type of counterpoint, in which the same music is repeated exactly by all the voices at different times. In the simplest sort of canon, the first voice sings or plays the tune, the next voice follows with the same notes a few moments later, and so on, until all the voices are singing. Rounds like *Frère Jacques*, *Three Blind Mice* and *Sumer is icumen in* are canons of this sort.

But a canon may be much more complicated than that – and in Bach's case it usually is. The second voice may sing the same music as the first, but upside down or back to front. The first method is known as Canon by Inversion, the second as Retrograde Canon. The other voices may even sing the tune both upside down *and* back to front – which takes great skill on the composer's part if the piece is not to sound chaotic. Alternatively, different voices may shorten or lengthen the notes of the melody in what are called Diminished and Augmented Canons. A canon with four voices might use two different melodies, or even four, rotating among the voices – and there may, of course, be more than four voices in a canon, though there are rarely more than six. Finally, voices 2 and 3 etc. may enter at different intervals (as in the Goldberg Variations), which considerably complicates the composer's task, because good canons obey not only the laws of counterpoint but also the laws of harmony.

If the essence of canon is strict imitation according to the rules, fugue adapts all these techniques in a freer way, applying the methods of canonic imitation to more than one tune. A fugue theme is traditionally called a subject. When the second voice enters, it restates this subject at a different pitch, while the first voice introduces a new theme, known as the countersubject. Then a third voice enters, and sometimes a fourth and fifth, and so on. The subject. and countersubject are restated in different ways, as in a canon – shortened, expanded, transposed – and, depending on the length and complexity of the fugue, other counter-subjects are introduced. There may also be what are called 'episodes', introducing new matter, although in strict fugues this music will usually be derived from the initial thematic material. Theoretically, there is no end to the proliferation of fugal countersubjects and episodes, but coherence usually limits them to one or two, and the formal principle behind fugue depends upon the highly disciplined working out of limited material. The composer's skill can be measured in three ways: by the elegance with which he fits the voices together, by the amount of variety he can extract from the simplest themes –

and most of all, by his ability to make these technically daunting achievements beautiful and even thrilling to hear.

Fugue is a much freer technique than canon, and historically more recent. Yet both already seemed stiff and antiquated in Bach's time. Polyphony had emerged from the urge to decorate and develop the austere lines of plainchant in medieval and Renaissance settings of the mass. But Bach lived in an increasingly secular age, when the opera house and concert room were displacing the church as centres of musical activity. The fashionable music of his time was essentially operatic: dramatic in form, and favouring the single accompanied melody over dense polyphonic textures. Yet the old forms still had plenty of life and drama left in them, as Bach was to show – and never more effectively than in our first piece.

Organist, doctor, theologian and Bach biographer Albert Schweitzer in about 1930.

Toccata in D minor BWV565

The Toccata in D minor (BWV565) is not only one of the most famous pieces of music ever written, but especially celebrated in the recording by Albert Schweitzer (1875–1965) reproduced here. An extraordinary man who eventually won the Nobel Prize for his medical work in Africa, Schweitzer was well qualified to understand Bach. Not only a distinguished organist and musical scholar, he was also trained as a theologian, and his book on Bach, published in 1905, is a fascinating study. Schweitzer belonged by achievement and by temperament to the heroic age, and his performances, though never extreme, are essentially romantic, underlining the spiritual and poetic qualities of the music.

The celebrity of this work makes it all the more ironic that recent research has cast doubt on its authorship. The Toccata was almost certainly written down by Bach, when the composer was about twenty, but there is now dispute about whether the piece is wholly original and how it reached the form in which we know it. Such debate is not really surprising when it concerns what is effectively a student work, particularly

The Trost organ at Altenburg which was tested and approved by Bach in 1739.

from a period in musical history when imitation, adaptation and even down-right plagiarism were common. What the scholarly doubts tell us is that the Toccata, though remarkable, is in style more characteristic of the period than of the composer, which is just what we would expect in the composition of a twenty-year-old, however gifted.

The Toccata certainly reveals many features common to the north German organ school: brilliant flourishes punctuated by dramatic silences, rapidly repeated notes, unison running themes in fast tempo, the invitation to use strongly contrasted organ-stops. The word 'toccata' means 'touched' and usually implies a piece which is rapid and delicate, a display of the player's dexterity. North German organists of Bach's time used the term more generally to indicate a virtuoso piece which was rhapsodic or improvisatory in manner. All these features appear in the work of Bach's early mentors: Böhm, Reincken and Buxtehude. The D minor Toccata also belongs to a form popular with these composers, the *praeambulum* or *preludium*, in which an extended movement is constructed from several distinct sections, linked thematically or connected by mood and dramatic contrast. Both structural devices can be found in this piece.

Whatever doubts there may be about authorship, there is nothing uncertain about the drama and brilliance of the Toccata, which is self-evidently the work of someone ambitious to show off his talents as composer and performer, full of vivid strokes and virtuoso passages. The first section opens with a call to attention: three miniature fanfares followed by a grinding *fortissimo* discord which resolves on a chord of D major. Then Bach introduces the scurrying figures so typical of a toccata, interrupted from time to time by great handfuls of chords and rapid scale passages. Eventually the section comes to rest on a chord of D minor, and there is a brief pause before the next section, a fugue on another toccata-like subject in busy semiquavers.

The fugue subject is a falling and rising scale of the simplest kind, filled out with repeated notes in a manner imitated from contemporary string music. The brilliant figuration sits easily under the organist's fingers. This jaunty music will remind many people more of Handel than of Bach – the Handel of all those dashing allegros such as *The Arrival of the Queen of Sheba*, in which essentially simple melodic and harmonic figures are worked up with tremendous verve into a musical soufflé. Bach's toccata is made of sterner stuff than that – there is anguish here, as well as delight – but the links between the two composers are clear.

This work is sometimes called 'Toccata and Fugue', as though it were in two clearly distinct sections, like the preludes and fugues in the *Well-tempered Clavier*. It is certainly true that many of Bach's early organ works pair a fugue with a less formal introductory movement. The dramatic effect of this pairing depends upon contrast between freedom and discipline, an impromptu prologue preparing the way for a tightly disciplined piece of counterpoint. No doubt this is exactly how many of the preludes came to be composed, improvisation being an organist's vital skill. But the Toccata in D minor is a rather different sort of work, a fantasia in which the fugue is actually one integral part. As if to make this point, Bach interrupts the fugue every so often with episodes which seem to have wandered in from the first section. Conversely, the fugue subject bears a close resemblance to a passage in the opening section. Thus the two sections are tied together. And the ending of the whole work is a magnificent *coup de théâtre* which abandons counterpoint entirely in favour of grand gestures, and constitutes what could be interpreted as a third section, as though the piece consisted of prelude, fugue and postlude – a common form at the time. As a final surprise, this noisy and boisterous piece is suddenly subdued, as if the frantic terminal scale passages had drained all the energy out of it. It then concludes on a most unusual cadence or closing chord sequence. Minor-key pieces written during this period conventionally finished on a major chord, but Bach's Toccata plumps firmly for the minor.

Passacaglia in C minor BWV582

The Passacaglia in C minor (BWV582) was probably composed towards the end of Bach's years in Weimar and it is one of the high points of his writing for organ. It bears some structural affinities with the Toccata in D minor, being a one-movement work dividing broadly into two parts, the second part a fugue, but there the resemblances end. While the Toccata is an extrovert, theatrical piece, the Passacaglia is one of Bach's most tightly argued masterpieces, compressing a complete conspectus of his contrapuntal art into less than fifteen minutes.

A passacaglia was originally a dance in triple time over a recurring bass line – a *basso ostinato* or 'obstinate' bass, known in English as a ground bass because it provides the ground on which the music stands. This is often four bars long; each statement of it is accompanied by different decorative lines above. The passacaglia is closely related to the chaconne – another dance in triple time over a ground bass – the difference being that a passacaglia is usually built on a tune, a chaconne on a sequence of harmonies (as, for example, in the last movement of Brahms's Fourth Symphony). A famous chaconne concludes Bach's violin Partita in D minor. There are many examples of both forms by Buxtehude and the French keyboard composers who influenced Bach, and he may have taken the first half of his eight-bar theme from a 'trio en passacaille' by the French composer André Raison – now, alas, remembered only for that loan.

Like most other passacaglias since the seventeenth century, Bach's work is not a dance, though it *is* in triple time. What matters to him, however, is the slow repetition of the ostinato theme twenty times after the initial statement on the organ pedals. Above this ground he constructs an increasingly complex web of counterpoint, concluding the piece with a splendid fugue. By using a theme of eight bars rather than four, Bach creates longer phrases and a much stronger sense of grandeur and solemnity than usual in such pieces. This allows him to build up and then release tremendous tension, a method of construction made all the more effective by the way in which Bach organizes the twenty variations, first dividing them into two groups of ten, which are then subdivided into groups of five. By doing this, Bach prevents the work from either breaking down into a mere series of short variations, or becoming a monotonous sequence of identically timed sections.

Furthermore, by dividing the variations into two groups of ten, Bach suggests, as in the D minor Toccata, a tripartite structure behind a two-part structure within a one-part structure! As a result, you can experience the form of this music in three different ways, separately or together: as a whole, as two parts (variations plus fugue), or as three parts (variations groups 1 and 2, plus fugue). For Bach, it is also an ingenious way of expressing in musical form a numerical relationship which articulates a theological doctrine of vital importance to him: the doctrine of the Holy Trinity, according to which God is three persons in one: Father, Son and Holy Ghost.

Bach was fascinated by the religious symbolism of mystical numbers and their multiples: ten for the commandments, twelve for the apostles, three for the Trinity, and so on. Moreover, as with the constraints of an exactly repeated bass and the symmetrical proportions it generates, numerical controls were a challenge to his ingenuity as a composer. 'In der Beschränkheit zeigt sich erst der Meister' said Goethe – the master reveals himself in his response to limitations. Bach is a perfect example of this dictum. It doesn't matter a jot whether or not the listener is aware of the number-work so long as he or she enjoys the music instinctively. But whether listeners know it or not, their pleasure in music is shaped by such numerical relationships; becoming conscious of them, if approached in the right way, is a stimulus to deeper understanding, not a barrier to appreciation. But what *is* the right way?

Perhaps the important thing to get clear is that numbers themselves may be important for composers but not for listeners. What matters to an audience is the effect of the numbers – and that means how they determine the way we hear the proportions, form and structure of a piece. Thus, we may be indifferent to Bach's obsession with the Holy Trinity – especially if we are not Christians – but, when we are at all sensitive to music, we cannot fail to become aware how important tripartite divisions are in his work. And repeated listening may reveal – as with the Passacaglia – that in his greatest pieces there is often a tension between different structural relationships, three set against two, two against one, and so on. This tension increases the power of the music – always provided, of course, that it is adequately articulated by performers and not merely muddled. Of course, we do not express such tension to ourselves in these dry numerical terms – but we do *experience* it. In this respect, talking about numbers is just one way of explaining audience reaction.

Yet, when all is said and done, what matters most to listeners is the beauty and power of music, however that is achieved, and no piece could be more beautiful and powerful than the Passacaglia. From its quiet, even unassuming beginnings, the listener is drawn along in the wake of the piece to its final majestic conclusion. We are a world away here from the rhapsodic manner of the Toccata. Indeed, comparison of the two works is an excellent way to get a sense of Bach's development from beginner to mature master.

Vor deinen Thron tret' ich BWV668

The comparison can be taken further by listening to the third organ piece on CD 3, the chorale prelude *Vor deinen Thron tret' ich* (BWV668). Probably the last piece Bach wrote, this was an adaptation of an earlier chorale prelude, *Wenn wir in höchsten Nöthen sein* (BWV641), which he included in the *Orgel-Büchlein*. Separated by more than thirty years, the two versions illuminate just how far Bach travelled in the last decade of his life. There is no display here, no grand gestures, grinding chords or swirling scales, as in the Toccata. Nor do we find the inexorable magnificence of the Passacaglia. All these features have given way to gentle understatement, as though the composer were communing with himself.

In the first setting of *Wenn wir in höchsten Nöthen sein* the tune is richly ornamented, like an aria or oboe solo from one of the cantatas, almost disappearing in the ornamental texture. The second setting of the tune, which has survived in two slightly different versions, drastically simplifies the ornamentation of the melody which is now clearly audible, but refines the counterpoint, so that each verse of the chorale is preceded by a canonic passage which combines phrases of the melody with their own diminished inversions. Whereas the earlier version proudly flourishes its keyboard virtuosity, the later version displays the sort of restraint which requires a lifetime's art to achieve.

It was presumably the contrapuntal ingenuity of this chorale setting which persuaded the composer's sons to use the second version (slightly amended) as a finale to the incomplete *Art of Fugue* when they published that work in 1751. But one wonders whether they were also aware of yet another aspect of their father's interest in musical symbolism present in *Vor deinen Thron*. C. P. E. Bach noted that the incomplete *Art of Fugue* breaks off just as Johann Sebastian introduces the family name as a theme. This is done by equating notes of the scale with letters of the alphabet, which produces in German musical notation the theme B♭—A—C—B♮. Bach used the device several times – in the Prelude and Fugue in B flat (BWV898), for example – and later composers, such as Liszt, incorporated the motif into their own music in homage to Bach. Carl Philipp Emanuel found the ending of the *Art of Fugue* touching, but he was dismissive of the technique that lay behind it. Yet a device called *gematria* is omnipresent in *Vor deinen Thron* and many later works. In the gematric system, each letter of the alphabet is numbered from 1 to 24 (I and J share the same number, as do U and V). Words are then given numerical values according to their totals, so BACH = 14, J. S. BACH = 41, and so on. As Karl Geiringer has pointed out, *Vor deinen Thron* has fourteen notes in the first line and forty-one in the complete chorale tune.

Carl Philipp Emanuel told Forkel that such dry stuff was of no real interest – and it must be said that the music itself is so gently and deeply affecting that technical complexity is the last thing we think of when listening to it. Yet the attitude to art revealed by a preoccupation with such techniques is profoundly important. For Bach, the 'harmony of the spheres' was no mere phrase but a reality embodied in mathematical relationships. Although it only becomes pervasive in his later work, numerology was not merely an old man's obsession but something which concerned him all his life.

Prelude and Fugue in E major BWV854

This concern affected the clavier music as much as the organ works. Bach nowhere mentions an equivalence between the twelve keys and the twelve apostles, but it is a parallel he must have been aware of when collecting the twenty-four preludes and fugues which make up the first book of the *Well-tempered Clavier*.

This compendium is one of Bach's most important works. A close look at the Toccata in D minor showed us that what seems to be a work in two distinct sections is, in fact, more complex. The *Well-tempered Clavier* appears at first sight to be altogether less complicated: twenty-four preludes followed by twenty-four fugues, making twenty-four pairs in all – a clear-cut pattern which is repeated in what has come to be known as Book II of the *Well-tempered Clavier* (though Bach did not give it that name).

In fact, the slightest study of this collection soon reveals a far more perplexing – and exciting – situation. Within the firmly organized framework there is extraordinary formal and technical diversity. As is often the case, Bach refined and rationalized the rambling and often chaotic musical forms he inherited from his predecessors; and in the *Well-tempered Clavier* he takes the rhapsodic praeambulum beloved of Buxtehude and others and brings it to order. Though the basic aesthetic principle of the form is a simple contrast between free introductory prelude and tightly argued fugue, Bach extracts astonishing variety from such contrast. Sometimes two very different movements are starkly juxtaposed. At other times they seem to blend into one another. There are occasions when Bach reverses the usual sequence and makes his fugue sound freer than its prelude. Alternatively, both prelude *and* fugue may be complex contrapuntal structures.

The Prelude and Fugue in E major from the first book of the *Well-tempered Clavier* is one of the most satisfying and least complicated pairings. It also illustrates Bach's unrivalled ability to create rich and beautiful music from the simplest material. Like others in the set, the theme of the E major prelude is based on no more than an arpeggio on the common chord. In this case, the arpeggio has a twiddle at the top which propels it through a series of melodic and harmonic transformations. This is a technique Bach uses in many of his chorale settings – most famously in *Jesu, Joy of Man's Desiring*, where very similar triplet figures decorate the chorale tune. In essence, the E major prelude is simply a series of spread chords, yet the effect is to suggest a

Title page to the autograph MS of the Well-tempered Clavier.

continuous stream of melody. The rocking triple time and gently changing harmonies evoke the pastoral style Bach found in Italian concertos of the period, and the piece might well be played on the clavichord.

The first bars of the three-voice fugue are, if anything, even more sparing of material, the opening subject consisting of an abruptly rising two-note figure, followed by scuttling semiquavers. This brisk little piece makes a good contrast to the smoothly flowing prelude, and the two appear to be well-balanced and complementary but quite different. A closer look suggests a more complicated relationship. The prelude, like the fugue, has three voices. Bach opens out his chord sequence to create a polyphonic texture, and the free imitation between right and left hands could almost persuade us we are listening to another fugue. One can also hear in the prelude anticipations of the fugue's sharply rising opening notes. Such thematic anticipations are not uncommon in the *Well-tempered Clavier*. Conversely, the fugue's tightly worked opening is followed by a loosening of the structure more commonly to be found in the Inventions. In other words, prelude and fugue are closer in both character and thematic material than they seem at first hearing, while managing to remain very distinct from one another.

Chromatic Fantasia and Fugue in D minor BWV903

This ability to contain variety within disciplined unity is nowhere more evident than in the amazing Chromatic Fantasia and Fugue in D minor (BWV903). Although the piece is free-standing, Bach might well have included it in the *Well-tempered Clavier* as a D minor specimen of the prelude and fugue form. One can see why he did not. For this work takes the principle of contrast to such extraordinary lengths that the piece threatens to fall apart. Yet by just staying whole it becomes one of the most remarkable pieces Bach ever composed. The Fantasia on its own can seem like an oddity, a bizarre one-off – especially to listeners who expect clockwork regularity and smoothness from Bach's music. The balancing fugue gives it perspective; even so, it would be hard to predict this music from the E major Prelude and Fugue or the Italian Concerto, though there are hints of it in the D minor Toccata.

But the Toccata is nowhere near as rowdy as the Fantasia and Fugue – especially when played, as here, by Wanda Landowska, one of the great interpreters of Bach. Landowska (1879–1959) was largely responsible for reviving the harpsichord in the early years of the twentieth century. Until then, Bach's keyboard works were played only on organ or piano. The tremendous performance she gives here on her own two-manual harpsichord underlines the capriciousness of the Fantasia, languishing and violent by turns, tentative one moment, the next throwing out cascades of notes like a dozen demented guitarists.

Landowska emphasizes the tense, mercurial, electric qualities of the music, and she is right to do so. For if the Chromatic Fantasia and Fugue strikes us as untypical of Bach, we are mistaken. Like the Toccata, it belongs to a kind of Baroque music well-established in the seventeenth century. Although we tend to think of Baroque art as monumental – recalling, perhaps, the palace of Versailles or St Peter's in Rome – we must remember that this monu-

Wanda Landowska (photographed here in 1909) led the revival of harpsichord playing and manufacture in this century.

mentality is essentially theatrical. The great palaces and churches of the seventeenth century are stages for the acting out of sumptuous rituals. Theatre penetrated deeply into Baroque art, and with it theatrical notions of display, performance, the contrast of illusion and reality, intensity of feeling and the exploration of extremes. The greatest Baroque art – the sculptor Bernini springs to mind – matches magnificence, clarity and grandeur with high drama and swirling emotion: exactly the qualities of Landowska's playing.

These pieces are 'chromatic' because they make extensive use of all twelve notes or colours of the scale and the exotic harmony – or rather, discord – which results from such use. This provides at least one link with the *Well-tempered Clavier*, for once again, Bach is exploring the nature of tonality and key-relationships. Chromatic display pieces were not unusual at the time, providing evidence of a composer's technical and expressive skill. Mattheson, Scarlatti, Gasparini and others all produced comparable works. But Bach, as usual, took the genre as far as it would go, pushing the very notion of tonality almost to breaking point. It is hard to say what key many bars of this piece are in. Once again, we are aware not only of strong feeling and virtuosity in his music: there is also a questing intelligence at work here, and a determination to exhaust the logical consequences of a musical idea.

Italian Concerto BWV971

In a less dramatic way, one might say the same of the Italian Concerto (BWV971), which explores the concerto form with equal rigour. It is a testament to Bach's versatility that the same man could compose the Chromatic Fantasia and Fugue and the Italian Concerto, a largely diatonic piece with few changes of key. And as if to rub the point home, the Italian Concerto was first published in 1735 as one item of the two which make up the *Clavier-Übung* II, the other being an Overture in the French Style (BWV831). It is as though the composer were determined to show that he was able to write superbly in any available style, which of course he was.

Where the Chromatic Fantasia and Fugue offers extremes of pathos and drama, the Italian Concerto provides just the opposite experience: here we find energy, sunny optimism, animal delight and well-being in the outer movements, calm confident tender lyricism in the slow movement. As Karl Geiringer has said, the work looks back to the concerto arrangements Bach made at Weimar, as though it were the transcription of an orchestral work which never actually existed. The obvious model is Vivaldi. Like Bach's preludes and fugues, the concertos Vivaldi produced in such profusion are based on a simple principle of contrast, infinitely varied. But if the prelude and fugue depend on contrast *between* movements, concertos require contrast *within* movements.

The outer movements of the Italian Concerto are structured like a concerto grosso, as indicated by the alternation of *forte* and *piano* (loud and soft), *tutti* and *solo* (all together and alone). These were carefully marked in the score by the composer himself, but they are evident anyway from the music. The work requires a large two-manual harpsichord to make its full effect, *piano* passages played on one keyboard, *forte* passages on the two keyboards coupled together. The central movement is an aria of the sort found in many of the cantatas, where a lyrical melody is treated to increasingly complex elaborations over a repeated bass. Bach uses the same method in the slow movements of his violin and harpsichord concertos.

Sarabande from Lute Suite in E minor BWV996

What must strike anyone listening to the slow movement of the Italian Concerto is the skill with which Bach adapts a melody designed for a sustaining string instrument to the short-breathed sounds of the harpsichord. The whole matter of instrumental character was one about which he thought deeply, as we can see from the music he wrote for lute. The most famous lutanist of his day was Bach's exact contemporary Sylvius Weiss who accompanied Wilhelm Freidemann on a visit to the composer in 1739. It cannot be shown that Bach wrote any of his extant lute music specifically for Weiss, though he composed several suites for the instrument.

The step from harpsichord to lute is not a long one technically: both are plucked string instruments. But the lute is an altogether more intimate medium than the powerful and brilliant two-manual harpsichord for which Bach composed his major keyboard works. Like the clavichord – sometimes said to have been Bach's own favourite keyboard instrument after the organ – the lute is gentle, quiet and private, a suitable medium for the performer to commune with himself. The influence of lute technique is reflected in several of the preludes from the

A Sarabande, 1716. Engraving by G. Lambranzi.

Well-tempered Clavier, e.g. the famous C major prelude from Book I with its softly rippling arpeggios, almost certainly better suited to clavichord than harpsichord.

Although the Sarabande from the Lute Suite in E minor is a grave and beautiful piece, some musicologists have wondered whether it is really by Bach. Played here on the guitar by Julian Bream, it sounds both idiomatic and characteristic of the composer. As with the D minor Toccata, arguments about the attribution of particular works, while important for scholars, are of interest to most listeners only insofar as they raise general questions about Bach's typicality and uniqueness. Was Bach's music representative of his time, or does it stand outside history? Presumably, the answer has to be: both. Bach's greatest music transcends its historical limitations in expressive power. On the other hand, he achieves that transcendence by working with the material and the musical outlook to hand. If the Sarabande is no supreme masterpiece, it nevertheless reveals the composer's complete understanding of an instrumental medium and an appropriate musical style.

Suite no. 3 in C major for solo cello BWV1009

The question of instrumental medium is raised intriguingly by another of Bach's lute pieces, the Suite in G minor (BWV995), which appears elsewhere in his output in a different key as a suite for solo cello. Which version came first? Nobody knows. The matter is of special interest because it has so often been remarked how superbly the six cello suites – though difficult – lie under the fingers. In all the suites, even nos. 5 and 6 which stand somewhat apart from the rest, Bach faces the same challenge – how to suggest interesting harmonic and contrapuntal textures with a solo string line – and he solves it with his customary brilliance. While listening to these suites one never feels that there ought to be more instruments playing. Indeed, the piano accompaniments added to the solo suites by Mendelssohn, Schumann and others, while historically interesting, only clutter the music.

The suite of dances (sometime called a partita) was a popular seventeenth-century genre which had become more or less standardized by Bach's time. He wrote suites for a range of solo instruments beside the cello – violin, keyboard, lute and flute – and four magnificent orchestral works in the same form. Once again, the basic aesthetic principle is contrast within overall unity. Each suite usually has a prelude (under a number of different names), followed by a sequence of dances. This sequence is not invariable, though most of Bach's suites contain allemandes, courantes and minuets. In addition, there may be bourrées, gavottes, gigues and other occasional movements. His suites – and sets of suites – also differ from one another in character. Among the keyboard works, for example, the French Suites are concise, light and elegant, while the English Suites are more serious and substantial, especially in their preludes – a movement lacking altogether in the French Suites, which always begin with the allemande. The character of the French Suites (not so named by Bach) may be explained by the fact that he included them in the collection of music he assembled for his wife, Anna Magdalena. The English Suites, on the other hand, seem to have been written with publication in mind.

As to the dances included, Bach himself refers in a letter to the different national styles in the music of his time, which may provide a clue. The allemande is a German dance, the gigue ('jig') an English one, the polonaise Polish, and so on. But all that remains of their national origins in Bach's work is the rhythmic structure, and that is really the point of them.

The unnamed cello suites are uniform in design but very different in character. They are all in six movements with the fixed pattern of prelude, allemande, courante, sarabande and final gigue. Only the fifth movement varies slightly from suite to suite. The fifth movement of the third suite in C major consists of two bourrées. Pablo Casals, who plays the work in this record-ing, suggested that each of the suites has its own distinctive character and that each suite takes its

Pablo Casals, photographed in 1937.

tone from the prelude: no. 1 is optimistic in mood, no. 2 tragic, no. 3 heroic, no. 4 grandiose, no. 5 tempestuous and no. 6 bucolic. His own performances are shaded accordingly.

An almost exact contemporary of Landowska and Schweitzer, Casals (1876–1973) played an important role in reviving the cello suites which are now central to the cello repertoire and to our understanding of Bach's music, and it is right that he should have the last word on their significance. According to his own testimony, Casals discovered the score in a second-hand shop.

> I did not even know of their existence, and no one had ever mentioned them to me. It was the great revelation of my life. I immediately felt that this was something of exceptional importance, and hugged my treasures all the way home. I started playing them in a state of indescribable excitement. For twelve years I studied and worked at them every day, and I was nearly twenty-five before I had the courage to play one of them in public. Before I did, no violinist or cellist had ever played a Suite in its entirety ... In those days these compositions were thought of as cold and academic works. How could anyone think of Bach as 'cold', when these Suites seem to shine with the most glittering kind of poetry?

CHAPTER 9
Ensemble Music

The second CD in this set is devoted almost entirely to Bach's concertos. What we would now call orchestral music did not bulk large in his output, and most of what there is appears in concerto form of one sort or another. Even one of the four orchestral suites – the Suite in B minor, reproduced here – is, to all intents and purposes, a kind of flute concerto. Fourteen harpsichord concertos survive, plus three for violin(s) and a number of works for other instrumental combinations – including, of course, the six Brandenburg Concertos. There are also several compositions entitled 'concerto' for solo instruments, notably the Italian Concerto and the keyboard pieces arranged from Vivaldi. Some of these works are transcriptions, others appear in two or more guises, and there were undoubtedly more which have been lost. These textual problems have led to much speculation about the first versions of Bach's concertos, and attempts to re-create them. The original works which survive, and which can be verified with some certainty, belong mainly to two periods of the composer's working life – the years at Cöthen (1717–23), and the early 1730s when Bach was providing music for his Leipzig collegium musicum.

It is sometimes said that the concertos of Bach's time are co-operative ventures between musicians playing together, while their romantic successors are essentially combative. Though it contains some truth, this distinction can be misleading. It has arisen in part from the complicated semantic history of the word 'concerto', which seems to make it mean two different things. On the one hand, it is thought to derive from the Italian verb *concertare*, which means 'play together'. On the other hand, it may descend from the Latin ancestor of that Italian verb which means 'contend' or 'dispute'. The meanings of these words appear to be opposite. But, as the linguistic relationship between the two verbs implies, this is not necessarily the case. Consider the meaning of another verb. When we *play* a team game we are both co-operating *and* competing; the two activities are reconcilable as long as we accept the *rules* of the game. The same is true in any ensemble music. The players in a string quartet are making a communal effort – but that effort involves discord as well as concord, dispute as well as consensus, and so on. In fact, we could say that a work's ultimate harmony derives at least part of its force from conflicts resolved, especially in such contrapuntal music as Bach's where there is a constant debate going on among the voices.

Another claim frequently heard is that the more combative nineteenth-century works emerge from the soloist's increasing need to display his or her talents as a star player in the wake of Paganini and Liszt. There is something in this claim, but once again we should not overrate it, for two reasons. Firstly, because, heard in context, many eighteenth-century concertos involve tremendous virtuosity on the soloist's part – Bach's Brandenburg no. 5, for example. And secondly, because the virtuosity of a soloist or group of soloists is often matched by the band in concertos of all periods.

The concerto originated in seventeenth-century Italy, where the term covered a range of instrumental and even vocal works; the seventh book of Monteverdi's madrigals is called 'Concerto'. It was from this diversity that the concerto grosso eventually emerged. As perfected by the Italian composers Torelli (1658–1709) and Corelli (1653–1713), the concerto grosso contrasts different groups of instruments. Typically, a small number of soloists (the *concertante* or *concertato*) is set against an accompanying band (the *ripieno*), supported by the continuo, usually consisting of harpsichord and a bass string instrument.

Torelli and his successors were more concerned with sound than with overall design; their concerti often have multiple movements but little sense of direction or structure. It was left to Vivaldi to reduce the concerto form to a conventional pattern of three movements – fast—slow—fast – though the design is by no means invariable. And it was Bach, under the influence of Vivaldi, who established the solo concerto by developing the concertato in ways undreamt of by his Italian predecessors. Vivaldi's instrumental music is essentially monodic – a single melodic line, accompanied and occasionally decorated. Most of his concertos, though tuneful and appealing, are too simple to bear repeated hearing – and many are frankly dull. This could never be said of Bach who succeeded in combining Vivaldi's brio with enriching polyphonic textures which are endlessly interesting. Even the Weimar arrangements of Vivaldi's own works are never mere transcriptions: they always improve on the originals.

Brandenburg Concerto no. 2 in F major BWV1047

Bach's concertos cover the whole range of contemporary forms from concerti grossi to full-scale virtuoso solo works, but most of his compositions in the genre come somewhere in between. The second Brandenburg Concerto in F major (BWV1047) is a case in point. Dating from about 1719, it was probably the earliest of the works on this CD to be composed. In style, this is a three-movement concerto grosso, with ripieno consisting of violins, viola and violone (or bass gamba), and concertato of oboe, recorder, violin and trumpet. All the musical interest is in the concertato parts, the ripieno providing no more than accompaniment – and even

Autograph MS from the first page of the Brandenburg Concerto no. 2.

this is omitted in the middle movement. The music of the outer movements is vigorous and intricately contrapuntal, weaving together a number of closely related (and eminently singable) themes, firmly based on the common chord of F major. The common chord basis and sharp rhythm of the opening theme evoke a military fanfare – no doubt suggested to Bach by his choice of trumpet; and because he uses the instrument in its highest register – the clarino – its penetrating tone inevitably makes the piece sound like a trumpet concerto at times.

The Andante second movement omits both trumpet and ripieno players. Recorder, oboe and violin are accompanied only by the continuo. The change of sonority is dramatic in any performance, the trumpet's absence a curiously positive stroke. After the brilliant textures of the first movement, the change of orchestration draws attention to the exquisite simplicity of the theme which is no more than a descending scale, slightly decorated, followed by a sighing figure. Bach achieves an astonishing diversity of tonal colour in this movement by revolving his thematic material through every possible combination of the three concertato instruments, and the piece is a model of economy.

The third movement – Allegro assai – reveals its own sort of economy in the variations it creates on a single rhythmic fanfare motif announced in the first bar, but such is the wealth of thematic material and the buzzing

The famous trumpeter and horn virtuoso Gottfried Reiche, who worked with Bach. Portrait by E. G. Haussmann, 1727.

energy of the music, that 'economy' is the last thing one thinks of.

As any listener can hear, no two of the Brandenburg Concertos are alike. Perhaps their most striking feature is the extraordinary variety of instrumental colour Bach extracts from his very limited palette. This is so even in the two concertos (nos. 3 and 6) which are for strings only. In no. 3 there are three groups of strings, each divided into three, and the work at times sounds very like a violin concerto. Brandenburg no. 6, on the other hand, is an ensemble work in which all the parts have equal value. The work omits violins altogether, opting for an unusual ensemble of two violas, two viole da gamba, cello and continuo, which gives it a wonderful dark, mellow colouring, at the opposite end of the tonal range from the brilliant second concerto.

As Norman Carrell has shown in his book on these works, all the instrumental parts are composed with the utmost care. A close study of the Brandenburg Concertos reveals the trouble Bach took to accommodate his players, even changing the shape of themes to suit instrumental capabilities. On the other hand, he clearly expected the highest standard of playing. The trumpet part in no. 2, for example, is exceptionally taxing, and each work presents different executive and interpretive problems.

Concerto in D minor for two violins BWV1043

The Concerto in D minor for two violins (BWV1043), which was also composed at Cöthen, might well have been added to the set of Brandenburg Concertos to which it is complementary. In this work Bach reverses the perspective of the second and third Brandenburg Concertos, which evolve the concerto grosso towards the solo concerto, by writing a concerto for two soloists which looks back to the concerto grosso.

The basic unit of construction for the fast movements of Bach's concertos – very evident in this work – is the *ritornello*. The word means 'little return' or refrain, and it refers to the recurrence of the opening music which appears in different keys during the movement, returning in the home key at the end. In between these passages there are contrasting episodes. This method was standardized in Vivaldi's concertos, and adapted by Bach who applies it in a far subtler manner. To begin with, he is more inclined than Vivaldi to modify the reappearances of the opening music by assigning it to different instrumental combinations, adding new contrapuntal parts, varying the harmony, or repeating only part of the opening statement.

As we have seen, Bach also develops the thematic material of his concertos contrapuntally in a manner foreign to Vivaldi. This is especially clear in the Concerto for two violins, the presence of two equal soloists inevitably suggesting dialogue if the violins are not simply to repeat one another or play in unison. Much of the writing for the two instruments is freely canonic. Close quasi-fugal imitation dominates the vigorous third movement, and the exquisite slow movement which has made this one of Bach's most popular works. The equivalent movements in Bach's two

A typical instrumental concert from the mid-eighteenth century.

other surviving violin concertos consist of elaborate melismas in which a thematic outline is filled in with filigree decoration. The same method can be found in the slow movement of the Italian Concerto. In the D minor Concerto, however, Bach builds the music from the intertwining of relatively plain contrapuntal lines accompanied by simple chords, and it is from this intertwining that the music derives its deeply affecting quality. The beginning of this movement is one of the most remarkable moments in music. The second violin outlines a descending scale in F major and then climbs up again to its starting-point. This is repeated by the first violin with decorations by the second. The process is repeated several times. Nothing could be simpler or more moving.

Concerto in C major for two claviers BWV1061
In 1736 Bach arranged the two-violin concerto for two keyboards and strings (BWV1062), transposing it into the key of C minor, possibly so that he could play the work with one of his sons. Another two-keyboard concerto in C minor (BWV1060) from about the same time is presumed

to be an arrangement of a concerto for violin and oboe, now lost. This work has been reconstructed for its original medium. There are also concertos for three and four harpsichords, all almost certainly arrangements from other sources. Some years before BWV1062, Bach had composed what seems to be an original work for the two keyboards, the Concerto in C major for two claviers (BWV1061) and we have included the last movement from this work in our selection. There is some evidence that the concerto was designed to be played without orchestral accompaniment. Unlike BWV1060 and BWV1062, it has relatively sketchy orchestral texture, and although the keyboard parts exist in Bach's autograph, the string parts do not.

The first movement is an impressive and substantial piece (at eight minutes, almost twice the length of many Bach concerto movements), and the slow movement, an Adagio ovvero largo in siciliano rhythm, is played without accompaniment. The last movement of BWV1061 is one of the most brilliant and exhilarating fugues Bach ever wrote. It certainly makes the present writer want to get up and dance round the room whenever he hears it – proof, if proof were needed, that a fugue need not be solemn. The two keyboards chase each other's tails in a long springing theme which comes in off the beat. As Karl Geiringer has pointed out, the fugue divides very clearly into four parts, each beginning with keyboards alone, bringing in the orchestra later for reinforcement. When the work is played on two modern pianos (as here) the peripheral nature of the band parts is even more pronounced.

Suite no. 2 in B minor BWV1067

A very different sound is provided by the orchestral Suite in B minor which may have been composed at about the same time as BWV1061. If so, Bach must have had a remarkable flautist among the players at his disposal. Like so many other cultural forms in the late seventeenth century, the orchestral suite originated in France where it emerged from the powerful operatic tradition developed by Jean-Baptiste Lully (1632–87). An Italian by birth, Lully started his career as a kitchen-boy but, by sheer force of character and talent, eventually became the most powerful musician at the court of Louis XIV. He established at Versailles a very distinctive operatic genre, including music, dance and magnificent scenery, which was influential throughout Europe.

Two of Lully's innovations were of particular importance. His operas (and all their French successors) conventionally open with preludes, or *ouverture*s, in which slow music in strongly dotted rhythms is followed by faster episodes and then by a restatement or reworking of the opening material. To satisfy the limitless demand for music to accompany all royal occasions at Versailles, these overtures were often detached from their operas. But Lully was also an accomplished dancer who made ballet and mime integral elements in an operatic tradition which survived in Paris until the end of the last century. French operas therefore contained dance episodes or whole balletic scenes, and it became a custom to extract the music of such episodes which, together with the *ouverture*, became a suite. Rather confusingly, such composite works were also known as *Ouvertures* and the form had a tremendous vogue in Germany in the early eighteenth century – hence, for example, the Overture in the French Style (BWV831) published together with the Italian Concerto.

By the time Bach came to compose his own four suites (*Ouvertüren* in German), the orchestral *Ouverture* was well-established. One hundred and thirty-five examples by Telemann survive, and he is known to have

Court musicians at Versailles painted in 1688 by François Puget. J. B. Lully is playing the lute.

written many more. French influence on Bach is evident in the style of the opening music and in the *Galanterien* – unusual character pieces – which supplement the conventional dances in these suites: a Forlane and Passepied in no. 1, the famous 'Air on the G string' in no. 3, a Réjouissance in no. 4, and the Rondeau, Polonaise and Badinerie of no. 2.

The Suite in B minor is the most typical and most perfect of Bach's works in this style, and the orchestration of solo flute and strings gives the piece an even more French colouring than usual – the flute being a favourite French instrument from that day to this. The work's fine texture is all the more evident if we compare it with, for example, the fourth suite, scored for full band with ceremonial oboes, trumpets and drums. The two are like a French soufflé and a German pudding.

The first movement of the B minor Suite falls into three distinct sections. After a grandiose opening which is repeated in the conventional way to give it extra weight, the central section is a lively *fugato* passage in which the syncopated rhythm of the first phrase gives the music an added lift. Despite the minor key, the light, bright colouring of the flute part (which demands great dexterity) gives an ethereal feeling to the music. This is followed by a slower conclusion in triple time, recalling the stately manner of the opening. Again the whole passage is repeated, so that this snatch of slower music appears in the middle of the movement as well as at the end. The repeats are important because they change the balance of the structure by making this effectively a movement of six sections, rather than three, lasting almost ten minutes.

The Overture is followed by a delicate Rondeau and Sarabande which recall the music of Bach's contemporary Couperin. A pair of sparky Bourrées precede a measured Polonaise, to which is added an ornate variation (called a *doublé*) for the flute. After a graceful Minuet, one of Bach's most entrancing inventions concludes the suite. The Badinerie (the word means 'playfulness') is constructed, as so often, from the simplest elements: a descending B minor arpeggio followed by a scurrying figure. From these plain materials Bach creates a wonderfully humorous little movement which makes a perfect ending to this lightest of orchestral works.

Clavier Concerto in F minor BWV1056

Bach's music is not popularly associated with humour – but only because popular opinion is wrong. The lively wit of the Badinerie's author also pervades the outer movements of the Clavier Concerto in F minor. It seems probable that this work was originally written for violin or oboe in a version now lost. Certainly, the slow movement in A flat (an adaptation of the sinfonia from Cantata 156) is a *cantilena* (flowing vocal melody) of the sort Bach wrote so prolifically for both instruments. In the cantata the melodic line remains relatively plain, but here the harpsichord, unable to sustain, fills in the melodic line with decoration over a bass line of plucked strings. As in Brandenburg no. 2, the rest of the band otherwise remains silent during the slow movement, which makes the entrance of bowed strings for the final cadence quite magical.

The first movement depends upon a simple but telling contrast. The four-square introductory 2/4 ritornello for orchestra circles obsessively round the tonic note F. At the end of this theme's first phrase there is a little triplet figure which the harpsichord echoes. This gives the cue for its own airy theme. The divergence between the earth-bound ritornello, constantly trying to escape from its one note, and the flighty harpsichord music is highly effective, all the more so because the two themes combine well, though quite distinct in sonority: brittle harpsichord versus substantial band. The effect is comic, or at least witty, as though the harpsichordist were desperately trying to escape from a bore who insists on making his point over and over again. The structure is reminiscent of the 'Goldenberg and Shmuyle' episode in Mussorgsky's *Pictures at an Exhibition*. And when the harpsichord finally seems to give in and states the opening ritornello on its own, three-quarters of the way through the movement, it cheekily dissolves the orchestra's sturdy music into its own triplets.

The very short, almost epigrammatic last movement – a Presto in triple time – is equally humorous in a rather different way. The main theme is syncopated, producing quirky cross-rhythms, and the abrupt final notes of each phrase in this theme – a falling fifth – are echoed on each appearance until they turn into a little tune by themselves. The harpsichord has music of its own, contrasted with the main ritornello, which also features a leaping fifth, this time rising rather than falling, as if to meet its mirror-image in the ritornello. The working up of a tiny detail in this way – and the fifth is the most basic of musical intervals – gives character to the whole movement. It is very typical of how Bach, thematically the most prodigal of composers when necessary, could also be the most economical. Because of its speed and shifting accents, this is not an easy piece to play, especially if taken too fast: in one famous recording it sounds as though all the musicians are running to catch different last buses.

Title and dedication to the first printed edition of the Musical Offering, *1747.*

'Ricercar à six' from the Musical Offering BWV 1079

We would not expect to encounter the kind of witty detail which characterizes the outer movements of the F minor Concerto in the *Musical Offering* Bach presented to the king of Prussia in 1747, just three years before his death. This contrapuntal masterpiece is a *tour de force* which explores one theme's polyphonic possibilities in a series of erudite canons and fugues. But we do find wit of another – and perhaps more significant – sort. In the previous chapter, I suggested that much of Bach's music draws strength from his ability to create diversity within unity, contrast within similarity. Conversely, one might also say that his technical virtuosity allows him to integrate the most diverse musical elements in what might seem to be the straitjacket of his contrapuntal manner.

A literary analogy may be useful here. According to the eighteenth-century critic Samuel Johnson (1709–84), wit can be thought of as '*discordia concors*; a combination of dissimilar images, or discovery of occult resemblances in things apparently unlike'. The notion of *discordia concors* is surely central to Bach's notion of polyphony in his last works, especially the *Musical Offering* which contains every available musical style and contrapuntal device from the most obscure canon to the most up-to-date sonata movement. And in the polyphonic devices of that work we are invited to discover innumerable 'occult resemblances' between different forms of the same theme.

One might compare Bach in this respect with another English writer (much admired by Johnson): his near contemporary Alexander Pope (1688–1744). All Pope's greatest work is written in heroic rhyming couplets, a highly restrictive medium. But, exactly like Bach, Pope exploits the limitations of his art to the full. The need to find rhymes, for example, is a positive spur to his powers of invention, while the tension between the couplet's tight form and the wide range of things Pope wants to express in it generates enormous energy. One could say the same of Bach's canons. In a poem like *The Dunciad*, written only a few years before the *Musical Offering*, the poet delights in finding 'occult resemblances' of every sort, not least in the founding idea of the poem, which is a comparison between bad art and sewage. This would certainly have appealed to Bach's own earthy sense of humour.

In view of the fact that the *Musical Offering* was one of the few works the composer published in his lifetime, it might seem ironic that there should be scholarly disagreement about the proper order of its constituent parts – and even about whether there *is* such an order. As Malcolm Boyd puts it:

> It is easy to forget that anyone who knocked on Bach's door in Leipzig in October 1747 and exchanged his thaler for a copy of the *Musical Offering* would have been given a sheaf of unbound and unstitched leaves, possibly in a loose wrapper or with the title-page bifolio acting as a temporary cover for the rest. If the purchaser had the misfortune to slip as he left Bach's

house and to scatter the pages of his copy over the cobbles of the Thomaskirchhof, he would have found some difficulty in rearranging them when he got home.

These unbound and unstitched sheets consisted of two fugues (called *ricercars* – because they are elaborately 'researched'), ten canons and a trio sonata, which is itself a substantial work in four movements lasting nearly twenty minutes. An additional problem is that Bach gives instrumentation only for the sonata and one of the canons, though the rest of the work is usually performed on flute, strings and harpsichord.

If we look closely at the *Musical Offering*, it is clear that Bach would not have minded such confusion. Indeed, on the evidence of the manuscript, he probably rather enjoyed it. Far from being a simple tribute to the king of Prussia, the *Musical Offering* presents interpreters with a number of other problems which make questions of order seem like minor matters. For Bach returns in this work to an ancient device known as the puzzle canon, in which the composer leaves the performer to work out exactly how the pieces are to be played. In two-part canons, for example, he may supply one voice and indicate where the second enters, but not at what interval, nor whether the second voice imitates the first exactly, backwards, upside down, etc. In one case even the second voice's entry point is missing. Instead the composer wrote on the score the words *quaerendo invenietis*: seek and you will find.

The variety of canonical techniques is extraordinary. Sometimes the theme is used as a cantus firmus round which two other voices imitate one another. In one canon the answering voice goes down when the leading voice goes up. Another begins in two parts and turns into three. A spiral canon revolves through a series of keys. A canon *per augmentationem contrario motu* uses both inversion and augmentation. There is a mirror canon and a crab canon in which one part repeats the other exactly – but backwards. As so often with Bach, these ingenious canons, intriguing in themselves, serve another purpose. The copy he sent to the king of Prussia was inscribed with Latin mottos at appropriate places. By the canon in augmentation he wrote *Notulibus Crescentibus crescat Fortuna Regis*: may the fortune of the king grow with the length of the notes. The ascending spiral canon is marked: *Ascendenteque Modulatione ascendat Gloria Regis*: may the king's glory grow with the rising modulation. On the first page there is an acrostic: *Regis Iussu Cantio Et Reliqua Canonica Arte Resoluta*: by order of the king the theme is resolved by canonic art. The initial letters of the Latin motto spell out the word 'ricercar'.

The first of the two ricercars is a diffuse piece bearing the marks of its origin in Bach's improvisation before the king of Prussia. The subject is padded out with the sort of conventional figuration all organists reached for when extemporizing. It is nevertheless a fine piece, but altogether inferior to the second ricercar, a magnificent fugue in six voices. Both can be performed on a keyboard instrument, but the second is more effective when scored for an instrumental ensemble, as here.

It has to be said that most listeners, particularly today, will probably not share Bach's interest in canons and similar arcane matters, but readers who find such devices intolerably artificial and academic might bear in mind the meaning of the word canon. A canon is a rule or set of rules. All art has rules. All art is artificial. The greatest artists, in Bach's terms, are therefore those who discover freedom in rules, nature in artifice, while they are bringing order to chaos and revealing the harmony of underlying law in the discord of appearances. As Pope puts it in his *Essay on Criticism*:

> Those RULES of old *discover'd*, not *devis'd*,
> Are *Nature* still, but *Nature Methodiz'd*;
> *Nature*, like *Liberty*, is but restrain'd
> By the same Laws which first *herself* ordain'd.

The rules of art are simply the laws of nature transposed into poetry, painting and music. Pope, like his contemporaries, was profoundly influenced by the example of Newton's work on gravitation and attraction. Newton was a deeply religious man who regarded his great discoveries as evidence of God's glory and His presence throughout creation. The laws of nature, in other words, as articulated in the rules of art, can be seen as a species of divine revelation. It is worth listening to the second ricercar in the light of this idea.

CHAPTER 10
Vocal Music

Singet dem Herrn BWV225

When Mozart visited Leipzig in 1789, he heard a performance of the motet *Singet dem Herrn* which made him feel that 'his whole soul seemed to be in his ears'. One can well understand why. This short choral work for eight voices divided into two choirs with instrumental accompaniment begins with a great shout of joy to the opening words from Psalm 149:

> Praise ye the Lord. Sing unto the Lord a new song, and his praise in the congregation of saints.
> Let Israel rejoice in him that made him: let the children of Zion be joyful in their King.
> Let them praise his name in the dance: let them sing praises unto him with timbrel and harp.

For most of its fifteen or so minutes the music glitters and gleams, bounding along in triple time, as though Bach had taken his cue from the psalmist's injunction to dance. Perhaps for this reason, *Singet dem Herrn* remained popular throughout the eighteenth century. Karl Geiringer quotes a letter to Goethe from the composer Carl Friedrich Zelter (1758–1832), Mendelssohn's friend and teacher, and one of the men behind the Bach revival. Zelter mentions how much the members of his choir enjoy performing *Singet dem Herrn* which, though difficult, is very satisfying to sing. It has continued in high esteem ever since, especially among singers.

The motet emerged as a distinct musical form in the thirteenth century. It uses a pre-existing melody with its own words as the basis (or cantus firmus) for a polyphonic choral work in which other melodies and words are added as counterpoints. At first, the primary melodies were taken from plainsong; in the fifteenth century Dufay introduced tunes from his own secular *chansons* into his motets, beginning a tradition which mingled sacred and secular music in complex combinations. After the mass, the motet was the dominant sacred choral form of the sixteenth- and early seventeenth-century church, and there are magnificent examples by Palestrina, Byrd and Victoria, not to mention hundreds of pieces by the great medieval masters from Machaut to Desprez. Motets were usually sung *a cappella* (unaccompanied) but often involved two choirs or a single choir divided into more than four parts. The richness of texture created by these divisions provided ample opportunities to display the composer's contrapuntal skill. The most spectacular example in English music is *Spem in alium* by Thomas Tallis (1505–85), which uses a choir of forty voices divided into eight 5-voice choirs.

Although the genre was already somewhat antiquated by his time, Bach was not the only member of his family to write motets. In the Lutheran Church, chorale tunes usually took the place of plainsong or secular melodies, and motets were often (though not always) accompanied, either by organ or, on special occasions, by band. Bach left six motets (including one of doubtful authenticity); he may have written more. The distinction between motets and cantatas is by no means clear-cut. The main obvious difference is that motets contain no arias or duets. To that extent, they are less dramatic, though Bach's extraordinarily resourceful choral writing more than compensates for any lack of textural contrasts. Malcolm Boyd suggests that the composer rated his motets less highly than his cantatas, basing this claim on the 1730 letter to the Leipzig council in which Bach distinguishes between the best singers, capable of performing cantatas, the worst, good only for simple chorales, and those in between who reach motet standard. But this distinction probably refers to the fact that many cantatas include virtuoso solo music, beyond the technical competence of all but the most gifted performers. There is certainly nothing *musically* inferior about *Singet dem Herrn*.

It was common to compose such works for festive occasions or for solemn ceremonies, such as the funerals of prominent citizens. The music was based on chorale tunes, which might also provide words, with extra text from the Bible, as in many of the cantatas. Bach treats his chorales in a variety of ways. In *Der Geist hilft unser Schwachheit auf* (BWV226) the chorale is sung complete, at the end of the work. In the far more ambitious *Jesu, meine Freude* (BWV227), which lasts three times as long as BWV226, the chorale opens and closes the work. In *Singet dem Herrn* (BWV225) it is broken into its constituent phrases and decorated.

This motet was probably written for the birthday of the Saxon Elector Friedrich August I, and first performed on 12 May 1727. Like other ceremonial pieces, it may therefore have been premiered in the open air before the house the elector occupied when in Leipzig. In form, it is rather like a little symphony, with three fast movements and one slow. After the initial call to attention, in which one choir sings emphatic chords embellished by the other, the long first part is fugal in character. The second, slower, section is based on the third stanza of the chorale *Nun lob mein Seel* ('Now bless my soul'), which derives in turn from Psalm 103:

Bless the Lord, O my soul: and all that is within me, bless his holy name.

The second choir sings verses of the chorale tune, while the first choir decorates it. The opening phrases of the decorative passages are related thematically to the chorale, its phrases shortened and quickened. The third movement – or 'scherzo' – of the motet, based on Psalm 150, returns to the brisk tempo of the opening, and the work concludes with a glorious fugal finale based on words from the same text. The long sinuous subject in triple time releases energy like a coiled spring unwinding.

'Seufzer, Tränen, Kummer, Not'

Bach's output of motets is dwarfed by the body of cantatas he produced. Not all of them survive. According to his Obituary, Bach wrote five sets of cantatas for the liturgical year, which means about 300 pieces in total. It seems possible that this is an overestimate and that he may only have composed three complete sets. Some of the cantatas in the collection he drew on for Sunday services at Leipzig were by other composers, and Bach himself recycled his own work for different occasions. Even so, almost 200 original church cantatas have survived, including 173 strictly liturgical works and several for special occasions. In addition, we have a number of secular cantatas. There may have been fifty or more of these, but again only a proportion remains.

The cantata originated in Italy during the early seventeenth century. The *cantata da camera* was a secular work, the *cantata da chiesa* sacred. Scoring varied greatly, though the combination of solo voice and continuo was popular. There are many examples for this medium by Handel and Alessandro Scarlatti (1660–1725), an important figure in the development of the cantata who wrote more than 600 examples. Characteristically, Scarlatti's cantatas include two or three arias separated by recitatives or *arioso* passages – a style of singing somewhere between recitative and aria. Some involve more than one singer, however, plus instrumental accompaniment and even choral parts, and it was these more extrava- gantly scored works which spawned the large-scale cantatas of the eighteenth and nineteenth centuries.

'Rehearsal for a Cantata'. Anonymous gouache, 1775.

By the beginning of the eighteenth century, the cantata – both solo and choral – was domesticated in Germany where it flourished at court and in church. No doubt Anna Magdalena Bach sang in cantati da camera at the courts of Cöthen, Zerbst and Weissenfels where she worked. By the time Bach began to compose, a conventional form was emerging for the cantata da chiesa. Shaped like an arch supported by three pillars, this form followed Scarlatti's favoured pattern of three arias or choruses, separated by recitatives. For more extended cantatas, the arch could easily be expanded to accommodate further pillars, and an opening sinfonia was often added to set the scene. The art of writing cantatas lay in varying the tone and texture within the overall theme; alternating the different elements of the work and balancing them against one another. There was thus a strong dramatic – and even theatrical – element in Bach's cantatas which is lacking in his motets, and which links them with the Passions.

Cantata 21, *Ich hatte viel Bekümmernis* (BWV21), from which we have taken one aria, is an example of the extended arch. This piece is formally problematic, being composed of eleven substantial movements divided into two parts. It is a massive and somewhat clumsy, if magnificent, cantata and scholars have suggested that it was cobbled together for a special occasion, actually being constructed from two pre-existing works. As a result, it appears to tell the same story twice. This does not prevent parts of the music from representing the youthful Bach at his best, including the opening sinfonia and the aria included here.

As the number suggests, *Ich hatte viel Bekümmernis* is an early work, written at Weimar in 1714 and later revised for performance in Leipzig in 1723 when it probably acquired its present cumbersome form. The identity of the librettist is not known and it may be that Bach himself assembled the text which is taken from two biblical sources. It has to be said that this text is rather confusing. Its first part, derived from the Epistles, is devoted to lamentation and the need to trust in God. 'I had a great affliction in my heart' is an approximate translation of the cantata's title and Bach varies this theme with extraordinary skill through six movements.

The five sections of part 2 are based on the parable of the lost sheep. These movements urge hope and patience on the creature and celebrate its return to the fold. Parts 1 and 2 fit together somewhat uneasily and might well be two separate cantatas. Further confusion sets in when the symbolism is extended from sheep to lambs in the final chorus, which sets the same text as Handel's 'Worthy is the Lamb'. The lost sheep found is somehow associated with the slaughtered lamb – or, rather, Lamb. Such associations – commonplace for eighteenth-century audiences – are more difficult for modern listeners to absorb, and may be one of the reasons for the relative unpopularity of the cantatas, which are not only devoted to expressing Christian doctrine but steeped in its symbolism.

There is no need, however, for any understanding of symbolism when we come to the aria, 'Seufzer, Tränen, Kummer, Not'. Beginning with the words 'Sighing, weeping, trouble, need, anxious longing, fear and death, gnaw my downcast heart', this is a deeply moving threnody and commentators have suggested that it reveals Bach learning from contemporary opera. In fact he might well have learnt the lesson of such expressiveness from secular cantatas. Though the text of the aria refers to a dark night of the soul, the highly charged music might serve equally well for the lament of an abandoned mistress. Scored for soprano, oboe and strings, the aria returns to the twisting chromaticism and discords of the cantata's opening sinfonia in falling figures which suggest the heavy load of grief. The way the oboe leans on the longer notes in its opening solo, which is then imitated by the singer, tugs at the heart.

Ich habe genug BWV82

Bach also composed many solo cantatas and one of the most perfect is *Ich habe genug* (BWV82). This is a good example of the arch form, three arias providing the pillars of the arch in Scarlattian style, with two recitatives between them. Scholars disagree about the dating of this cantata, which most put somewhere between 1727 and 1732 though some of the material appears earlier still. In Anna Magdalena's 1725 *Notenbuch* we find a recitative and aria for soprano which use the same music as sections 2 and 3 of this cantata, which might suggest that *Ich habe genug* predates the Notebook. There is a different and more intriguing possibility, however. Very strikingly, the aria was copied into the book not once but twice. Furthermore, it is the only time music from the church cantatas appears in the Notebooks, which suggests how highly Bach or someone else – perhaps Anna Magdalena herself – must have valued it. It may therefore be the case that Bach, knowing how much his wife loved the music, determined to use it in a work which turned out to be one of his most beautiful and perfect pieces.

Ich habe genug was written for the Feast of the Purification of the Blessed Virgin Mary, and the text refers to the Song of Simeon in St Luke's Gospel ii. 22–34. The Holy Ghost reveals to Simeon that he will not die before he has seen Jesus Christ. Having seen the child, he says

> Lord, now lettest thou thy servant depart in peace, according to thy word . . .

The cantata, which expands on Simeon's words, is therefore a form of Nunc dimittis, a petition for dismissal. The work is scored for bass voice, oboe, strings and continuo. The music opens with a syncopated, rocking string figure over a falling bass. The oboe then plays the dotted rising and falling theme which anticipates the vocal part. When the voice enters the oboe plays arabesques, resulting in a satisfying richness of texture from the three parts. The opening words of the cantata are 'It is enough. I have taken into my longing arms the Saviour, the hope of the pious.' The theme is resignation to God's will at the imminence of death, and the rocking string music seems to suggest on the one hand the calmness and stability bestowed by trust in the Lord, and on the other the downward pull of death which – as the syncopations and discords hint – is nevertheless still alarming. But, as the following recitative insists, 'Ich habe genug': it is time to depart.

It was the second aria, 'Schlummert ein', which Bach copied into his wife's Notebook. This is a heavenly lullaby to the words 'Fall asleep, ye weary eyes, close softly and blissfully.' The strings state the instantly memorable opening melody, which is then repeated by the voice. The oboe is silent throughout. The last phrase of the main theme – a syncopated falling scale – is especially striking. Unusually, this movement is a rondo, which means that one waits impatiently for the heavenly opening to return – or would do, were the episodes between the statements of the main theme not so fine.

The second aria forms a transition between the subdued agitation of the first aria and the joy of the last. The second episode of the rondo explicitly contrasts the misery we must endure through death in this world with the peace that death brings us in the next. The aria is followed by a magical recitative – magically sung here by Hans Hotter, despite the rather over-scored accompaniment – to the words 'My God! now comes the beautiful moment when I shall journey in peace, and rest with Thee, in the dust of cool earth, there in Thy bosom.' Then, as the voice sings 'World, goodnight', the continuo descends two octaves to a low C, as if to suggest submission.

In the third aria, the agitation of the first and the calm of the second are displaced by joy. Decorated with a florid arabesque, the word 'joy' recurs three times, at the beginning of each section. 'Ich freue mich auf meinem Tod' sings the bass: 'I look forward to my death.' Marked *Vivace*, the vigorous opening 3/8 orchestral theme based on a rising scale is the antithesis of the first aria's drooping music. The downward pull there is matched here by an insistent upward movement. As Whittaker observes, the significance of these flying passages becomes clear when the text later refers to the soul escaping from the world's suffering to which it has been bound so far.

Schweigt stille, plaudert nicht BWV211

Nothing could be further from *Ich habe genug* in mood, approach or purpose than Cantata 211, *Schweigt stille, plaudert nicht*, usually known as the 'Coffee' Cantata (BWV211). This is a secular work with a text by Bach's friend Picander. Where Cantata 82 is stately, spiritual, lyrical, tender and finely wrought, the 'Coffee' Cantata is mercurial, episodic, cheerful and even cheeky. Scored for three singers – soprano, tenor and bass – accompanied by a band of strings, flute and continuo, this work was written in 1732, and was very well suited to a lively evening in Zimmerman's Coffee-House where it was presumably performed by Bach's collegium musicum.

A satire on the coffee craze which swept Europe in the late seventeenth and early eighteenth centuries, the text also celebrates a traditional comic theme: the ability of women to get what they want, however fierce the male opposition. It may well be that – as often happened in comic works at this time – the soprano part was sung by a falsetto male voice, broadening the burlesque effect still further. For, as the plot makes clear, the 'Coffee' Cantata is a miniature *opera buffa*. Old Schlendrian (bass) – the name means something like 'Humbug' – laments the fact that his daughter, Lieschen, is addicted to coffee. In desperation, he refuses to find her a husband unless she gives it up. Reluctantly, she agrees to do so. The drama ends with father and daughter reconciled, as Lieschen looks forward to marriage.

At least, that is how Picander's original libretto concludes. But someone – possibly Bach himself – added two numbers which give a decidedly saucy and rather more realistic turn to the action. Having outwardly accepted her father's commands, Lieschen privately spreads the news that she will only accept a man who allows her to drink coffee after marriage – which will thus, at a stroke, free her from Schlendrian's tyranny, provide the pleasures of the marriage bed and leave her free to indulge her original addiction. Listeners are left in no doubt that Lieschen is a creature of strong appetites.

The music of the 'Coffee' Cantata is instantly appealing and wears its considerable ingenuity with the lightest of airs – for even here Bach pays meticulous attention to every detail. The cantata parodies the Passions in form – thus reversing a process by which he often adapted secular material to sacred means, as for example in the B minor Mass (see below). A narrator or 'Historicus' sung by the tenor introduces and closes the story, joining with the other two singers in the final chorus reproduced here. Each character has two arias, interspersed by recitatives in which they converse. The final chorus is like a rondo or a dance with two trios in form, three statements of the main theme being separated by two episodes. The theme itself is appropriately rustic and vigorous, and sharp-eared listeners may notice that it falls into phrases of *six* bars, rather than the conventional eight, very like a nursery-rhyme, which partly accounts for the music's very perky, quirky manner. According to the text: 'Die Katze lässt das Mausen nicht, die Jungfern bleiben Kaffee-Schwestern' (Girls will drink coffee together as long as cats chase mice). In the manner of opera buffa, Schlendrian and Lieschen step out of their roles to sing the chorus, joined by the tenor Historicus, while insistent rhythms and melodic shapes underline the inevitability of the eternal truths they intone.

Mass in B minor BWV232

A rather different sort of eternal truth is the subject of what many people regard as the summit of Bach's achievement, the Mass in B minor. This work is sometimes compared with Beethoven's Ninth Symphony and even with Wagner's *Parsifal*. All three come near the end of their composers' careers, all three are massive and sublime, all are (in different senses) religious, presenting a comprehensive spiritual and musical vision. According to this view, the Mass is a synthesis of Bach's musical wisdom, a fitting summation of his faith and his art and the relationship between them. As Carl Zelter put it, the Mass in B minor is 'probably the greatest work of art the world has ever seen'.

Not everyone agrees with Zelter. It has also been suggested that, while there are many magnificent movements in the Mass, the whole work is rather a rag-bag. Critics point out that the movements vary considerably, not only in quality but in style, and that many are adapted from secular compositions, which appears to undermine the claims of those who see in this work a consistently inspired masterpiece. As for its religious significance, they note that this is a Catholic work written to please a patron; that Bach was a Protestant who committed his inmost thoughts elsewhere; and that the music was never anyway intended for performance, being unsuited to liturgical use in either rite.

Both viewpoints can be exaggerated and both contain misconceptions. All composers adapt music from one work to another. Such adaptation – or 'parody', as it is usually called – was especially common in the early eighteenth century when composers were under pressure to produce huge amounts of music very quickly. There is also evidence that Bach assembled the constituent parts of the work with great care, as he did with other late portmanteau pieces. Complex number symbolism governs the disposition of the sections in relation to one another, the proportions of individual parts, and the contrapuntal devices used within them.

Nor are differences of style within a work necessarily significant. Every work of art, however distinctive or well-integrated, shows the influence of other works. The B minor Mass is no more striking in this respect than masses by Schubert and Mozart which draw on a range of styles and techniques from old-fashioned fugue to modern symphony. And the circumstances which bring a work of art into being may be as irrelevant to its value as the materials from which it was created. Many sublime masterpieces have been written for vile patrons, and even, alas, by vile composers – *Parsifal*, for one.

Analogies with Beethoven and Wagner, on the other hand, are certainly misleading. If they have to be made, the *Missa Solemnis* would offer a better comparison with the Mass in B minor. Both were written over a long period and suggest composers struggling to integrate different styles and technical modes into a single form. But even that comparison exposes differences rather than similarities. Though both are grand in scale, these settings of the mass differ formally, emotionally and dynamically. Beethoven's music, however monumental, is always on the move, always going somewhere. But Bach – just as full of life and energy as his great successor – creates static Baroque forms whose drama is essentially statuesque and gestural. We might say that, whereas in Beethoven's music we are always eager to know our destination, making the journey is what counts in Bach.

On one point both sides often agree, namely that the Mass in B minor was never intended for performance. Certainly, it was unusual in this period to perform a liturgical work outside a liturgical context. But what critics usually mean is not only that the Mass *could* not be performed, but that it was never *meant* to be. It is thus classed with other late works – the *Well-tempered Clavier* (Book II), the *Art of Fugue*, the *Musical Offering* – which supposedly reflect the composer's growing obsession with working out contrapuntal problems on paper. I do not accept the notion that

Bach's late works are somehow impractical – which is often put forward by people who do not flinch at the thought of the *Grosse Fuge* or a five-hour Wagner opera. All Bach's music was meant to be heard. Andrew Parrott makes the work's musical credibility admirably clear in the performance we reproduce, by balancing sublime and monumental aspects – as found, for example, in the heart-rending *Crucifixus* – against the lyrical and dance-like qualities which characterize so many of the movements.

The tendency to put the B minor Mass on a pedestal of its own is perhaps a survival of the romantic attitudes to Bach described in the introduction to this book. Such attitudes encourage us to see artistic careers – and indeed their products – in terms of heroic struggle which reaches a climax towards the end. But Bach does not fit this pattern. It is true that he continued to develop technically as he aged, but a search for the sort of spiritual deepening some people claim to find in Beethoven's later work is quite beside the point. *Vor deinen Thron* (BWV668), which was written in the last weeks of Bach's life, derives every note from augmentations and diminutions of the theme. It is a technical advance on anything the young composer might have written, but the faith it expresses was lifelong and unchanging. Spiritually, Bach ended where he began.

Parrott's recording of the B minor Mass also provides an invigorating corrective to over-romantic views of Bach. It is 'authentic' in two important ways. First, because it deploys the sort of forces Bach might have used himself. Until very recently, the major choral works – the Mass and the two Passions – were performed by large orchestras and even larger choirs on the assumption that big works must demand big forces. Here we see the analogy with Beethoven and Wagner at work again (and the same principle applies, of course, to Handel's oratorios). But Bach had only a small instrumental and vocal ensemble at his disposal, and it seems likely that instrumentalists often outnumbered vocalists. As Hugh Keyte remarks in a note written to accompany the original issue of this recording:

> Joshua Rifkin has recently argued that Bach's Leipzig cantatas were norm-
> ally performed by only four singers, who took the chorus as well as solo

parts. When more singers were available, Bach would either write in eight parts (as in the motets and the *St Matthew Passion*) or else treat his four extra singers as ripienists, using them to strengthen the four concertists in choruses.

Andrew Parrott's performance of the Mass uses seven soloists who are joined by five ripieno singers in the full choral sections, whereas the band consists of twenty-four players. The effect is to sharpen and lighten the vocal texture. This is a world away from the (authentically) massive sounds of the *Missa Solemnis*.

Authenticity also prevails in the choice of tempi and instrumentation. Big choral and orchestral forces inevitably tend to slow the momentum of a performance. Even if the actual speed is fast, it can *feel* slower than it is because of the thick sound they create. A much reduced choir and orchestra not only promote faster speeds: by thinning the texture they enhance further the sense of movement. And the use of old instruments produces a clean, clear sound in which all the lines can be heard. Modern orchestras work at blending instrumental groups into a unified ensemble. Letting light and air into the band, as it were, relieves the weight which bore down on many older performances.

Which is not, of course, to deny the possibility of other performance styles. I began this book by contrasting two approaches to Bach, the romantic and the authentic. Needless to say, this contrast is a gross simplification. I did not make it in order to praise one style and condemn another, but to suggest that there are – broadly speaking – two ways into music: one seeks to re-create the work 'as it was', the other to re-create it as it might be. Both can be valid. Schweitzer and Landowska show that the romantic way can be profoundly illuminating, while Parrott and Jacob make us hear the music anew. By the same token, both approaches have their faults. If ersatz romantics are inclined to mistake soggy emotionalism for spiritual profundity, their authentic successors some-times confuse the genuine with the merely dreary. Fortunately, neither fault affects the recordings on these CDs.

The Mass is divided into four sections: Missa, Creed, Sanctus and Osanna. The last two are reproduced here, representing approximately one fifth of the work. Bach does not follow conventional divisions of the text (which, in the Catholic Church, involves five parts – Kyrie, Gloria, Credo, Sanctus and Agnus Dei). Instead he divides his text into twenty-five numbers. Only the Sanctus remains as it is in conventional use. The music for this movement was originally written in Leipzig for Christmas, 1724. Firmly rooted in D major – traditionally the key of ceremonial music with trumpets and drums – the movement is an extended chorus in two parts. The first section sets the words: 'Sanctus, sanctus, Dominus Deus Sabaoth' (Holy, holy is the Lord God of Hosts). Its stately music opens in duple time with a fanfare figure of the sort we have encountered before – a falling third, followed by a running triplet figure – while the orchestra accompanies in dotted rhythms over a slow, persistently repeated bass figure. In one form or another, these three motifs provide the material for the whole section. The choir is divided into six parts – two sopranos, two altos, tenor and bass – and the Sanctus is the only movement in this performance which deploys its full vocal forces.

The livelier second section sets the rest of the words: 'Pleni sunt coeli et terra gloria ejus' (Heaven and earth are full of His glory). Whereas the first section frequently divides the choir into two groups, the second section emphasizes the independence of the voices. Taken together with the change from duple to triple time, this increases the sense of rising excitement. The effect is underlined further by the subtle thematic linking of the two sections: the triplet rhythm from the first becomes the basis of the theme in part two.

Taking up the tempo and the triple time from the second half of the Sanctus, the Osanna ('Osanna in excelsis': Hosanna in the highest) is in what one might call the composer's Vivaldi manner. The opening unison call to attention, like the long orchestral coda, might be taken from one of Bach's Weimar concerto arrangements. The Osanna is sung twice – before and after the Benedictus ('Benedictus qui venit in nomine Domini': Blessed is he that cometh in the name of the Lord). The tonal contrast between the two movements is complete, the choir and orchestra falling silent in the Benedictus which is scored for tenor and continuo with a wonderful flute *obbligato*. Flute arabesques recall the Suite no. 2; both works are in the key of B minor.

The angular chromatic line of the following Agnus Dei for contralto may remind listeners of 'Seufzer, Tränen, Kummer, Not'. Given that work's association with lambs the link would be appropriate. 'Agnus Dei qui tollis peccata mundi, miserere nobis' – Lamb of God, that takest away the sins of the world, have mercy on us. The Agnus Dei moves from the standard D major/B minor/F sharp minor tonality of most movements in this work towards a surprising G minor. This intensifies the strangeness and desolation of the music. More importantly, it makes the return to D major in the final movement seem all the more satisfying and conclusive.

After the anguished chromaticism of the Agnus Dei, the Dona nobis pacem (Grant us peace) is largely diatonic, the subject of its fugue moving in smooth steps. If the music – especially the rising opening phrases – sounds almost medieval, that is not surprising. Several movements in the Mass are based on Gregorian chants, notably the Credo. The gravely beautiful Dona nobis pacem appropriately recalls the great medieval and Renaissance masters to whose contrapuntal skill all Bach's music pays tribute. But as readers acquainted with the Mass will know, the music of the Dona nobis pacem is not unfamiliar: in a complete performance we would already have heard it sung to different words much earlier in the work, as the central section of the Gloria: 'Gratias agimus tibi propter magnam gloriam tuam' – We give Thee thanks for Thy great glory. Why does Bach use this music twice – and why here? Clearly, he means us to associate these two sections with one another. If we put the two ideas together – praising God for His glory and beseeching Him to grant peace – we are immediately reminded of the famous phrase from Dante's *Divine Comedy*: 'E'n la sua volontate è nostra pace'. In His will is our peace. What motto could be more appropriate for the whole of Bach's life and work?

Further Reading

There is an extensive and growing Bach literature. Listed below are some of the more accessible books in English.

Biography

Bach's first biographer, J. N. Forkel, is still worth reading, if only for his delightful anecdotes. The book has been translated into English twice, the second time by C. S. Terry whose own *Bach: a Biography*, Oxford University Press, 1967, is still the standard English life of the composer, revised several times since first publication in 1928. Philipp Spitta's magisterial *Johann Sebastian Bach*, London, 1884–5, is still a resource for biographers. Among more recent works, Karl Geiringer's *Johann Sebastian Bach*, Allen and Unwin, 1967, is the most readable and comprehensive. Whereas Terry concentrates on biography, Geiringer provides an introduction to the music, as does Malcolm Boyd's Bach volume for the Master Musicians series published by J. M. Dent in 1983 and reprinted by Oxford University Press in 1995. Boyd is briefer and more up to date than Terry and Geiringer, but he is also more detached and technical. His book includes a helpful chronology and list of works. For readers interested in the Bach clan and J. S. Bach's place in it, Percy Young's *The Bachs 1500–1850*, J. M. Dent, 1970, and Karl Geiringer's *The Bach Family*, Allen and Unwin, 1954, both make fascinating reading. Finally, there is *Bach's World*, Indiana University Press, 1970, by Jan Chiapusso, which describes the intellectual and religious milieu in some detail.

Criticism

Geiringer and Boyd have illuminating things to say about the music. Geiringer is especially good on the organ works, Boyd on the theoretical context. C. S. Terry's *The Music of Bach*, Oxford University Press, 1933, written as a companion volume to his biography, is still useful. Among specialist works, the following are all lucid and helpful: Peter Williams,

The Organ Music of J. S. Bach, 3 vols, Cambridge University Press, 1980–84; W. G. Whittaker, *The Cantatas of Johann Sebastian Bach*, Oxford University Press, 1959; D. F. Tovey, *A Companion to the Art of Fugue*, Oxford University Press, 1931; and Norman Carrell, *Bach's Brandenburg Concertos*, Allen and Unwin, 1963.

Further Listening

Keyboard Music

One might begin with the delightful Inventions in two and three parts (BWV772–86 and 787–801). Then the two sets of French and English Suites, which are very different in character. Among the finest are the G major French Suite (BWV816), and the F major English Suite (BWV809). The Partitas in B flat (BWV825) and D (BWV828) are equally good. Between them, these four works offer every imaginable variation on early eighteenth-century dance forms.

The two books of *The Well-tempered Clavier* (BWV846–93) provide a different kind of musical experience. One can listen to each book complete, but it is probably wiser to browse like Stravinsky, who used to begin each day's composing in his later years by playing through a prelude and fugue at the piano. My own favourites are Book I: C minor, D major, F♯ major, A♭ major and B minor; Book II: C major, E♭ major, G minor and B♭ major.

The Goldberg Variations (BWV988) repay continued listening, either as a whole or in parts. The theme and the easier variations (including 2, 4, 6, 10, 18 and 19) are within the competence of pianists with a very modest technique, as are many Inventions and dances from the Suites, and the simpler preludes from the *Well-tempered Clavier*.

Organ Music

It isn't easy to choose from the wealth of organ music, but the following 'free' pieces are all superb and easy to find on record: 'Dorian' Toccata and Fugue in D minor (BWV538), Toccata and Fugue in F (BWV540), Fantasia and Fugue in G minor (BWV542), Prelude and Fugue in C minor (BWV546), Prelude and Fugue in E minor (BWV548), Prelude and Fugue in E flat (BWV552) and six Trio Sonatas (BWV525–30).

All the 140 or so chorale settings are of interest in one way or another. One might begin with the so-called 'Leipzig' chorales (BWV651–67) Bach composed early in his career and revised late in life. Then the 'Schübler' collection (BWV645–50), and the pieces published in *Clavier-Übung* III (BWV669–89). Anyone who wants to see how Bach treated the same tune in different ways might consider the various settings of *Nun komm, der Heiden Heiland* – BWV599, 659–61 and 699 – and *Vom Himmel hoch* – BWV606, 700, 701 and 738. Finally, there are the late and extraordinary Canonic Variations (BWV769), also based on the tune of *Vom Himmel hoch*.

Instrumental and Ensemble Works

After the Suite in C for solo cello, the other suites which complete the set of six (BWV1007–12) make superb listening, as do the unaccompanied violin sonatas and partitas, especially the Partitas in D minor and E major (BWV1005 and 1006). The authorship of several Bach flute sonatas is now disputed but it seems certain that he did write the best of them in B minor (BWV1030), which has an especially fine first movement. The Concerto for two violins is an excellent introduction to the surviving works for solo violin and orchestra (BWV1041 and 1042). In the same way, one might follow up the second Brandenburg Concerto with the brilliant no. 4 (BWV1049) and – at the opposite tonal extreme – the lyrical, dark-hued no. 6 (BWV1051). The most popular of the orchestral suites is probably BWV1068 which contains the famous 'Air on the G string'. Personally, I prefer the magnificent Suite in C (BWV1066).

The history of the harpsichord concertos is complicated. The works in D minor (BWV1052) and A major (BWV1055) are both very fine, and the rest all have delightful movements. For those who can read music, miniature scores and piano versions of all these works are available.

Vocal Music

Essential for explorers of Bach's vocal music are the rest of the Mass in B minor (BWV232) and the *St Matthew Passion* (BWV244). On the other hand, listeners to these complex, searing and enormous works might benefit from previous acquaintance with the motets and cantatas. Of the motets, *Der Geist hilft unser Schwachheit auf* (BWV226) and *Jesu, meine Freude* (BWV227) are both very fine. More than two hundred cantatas survive and readers who want to explore them in detail are advised to seek guidance from the book by Whittaker mentioned in 'Further Reading'. Among the secular works, *Was mir behagt* (BWV208) and the 'Peasant' Cantata – *Mer hahn en neue Oberkeet* (BWV212) – are charming, the one lyrical and lively, the other comic. It is hard to choose from the sacred cantatas, but deservedly popular works include *Jesu, der du meine Seele* (BWV78), *Ein feste Burg ist unser Gott* (BWV80), *Christ lag in Todes Banden* (BWV4), *Mein Herze schwimmt im Blut* (BWV199), *Wachet auf* (BWV140) and *Gottes Zeist is die allerbeste Zeit* (BWV106).

There are two other sorts of music which illuminate Bach's career. First, the work of contemporaries and predecessors, including his sons, especially the tortured Wilhelm Friedemann – the greatest among them – and the suave Johann Christian, who met and influenced Mozart. Their music is not easy to find on record, but well worth looking out for. The works of composers whom he adapted and arranged – principally Vivaldi and fellow Italians – and composers who influenced him – notably Buxtehude – are rapidly becoming more easily available on CD.

Finally, there are the arrangements of Bach by composers from his time to ours. These constitute a musical genre in themselves. Especially worth searching out are Busoni's stunning piano transcription of the Chaconne in D minor and Stravinsky's version of the Canonic Variations.

Chronology

DATE	LIFE AND WORKS	MUSICAL CONTEXT	HISTORICAL BACKGROUND
1678		Birth of Vivaldi.	
1681		Birth of Telemann.	
1683		Birth of Rameau.	Turks besiege Vienna.
1685	Johann Sebastian Bach born 21 March at Eisenach.	Birth of Handel and D. Scarlatti.	Revocation of the Edict of Nantes (France).
1687		Death of Lully (45).	Newton's *Principia Mathematica*.
1688			Death of the 'Great Elector' Frederick William of Brandenburg. 'Glorious Revolution': James II deposed by William and Mary (Great Britain). War of the League of Augsburg (to 1697).
1689		Purcell: *Dido and Aeneas*.	Bill of Rights (Great Britain). Devastation of Palatinate by French army.
1692	Enters Lateinschule, Eisenach.		Duchy of Brunswick-Lüneburg ('Hanover') becomes an electorate.
1694	Mother (50) dies, 1 May.		Voltaire born. University of Halle founded.
1695	Father (49) dies. JSB lives with brother, Johann Christoph (24) in Ohrdruf.	Death of Purcell (36).	
1697			Friedrich August I, elector of Saxony, converts to Catholicism and becomes king of Poland. Peace of Ryswick.
1699		Birth of Hasse.	Treaty of Karlowitz: Hungary reclaimed from Ottoman Empire.
1700	Studies at Michaelisschule, Lüneburg.		Great Northern War (to 1721). Birth of the poet Gottsched.
1701	Walks to Hamburg to hear Reincken.		Elector of Brandenburg crowned King Frederick I of Prussia. Berlin Academy founded. War of Spanish Succession (to 1713).
1703	Court musician at Weimar. Organist at Arnstadt. Capriccio in E.		Building of St Petersburg begins.
1704	*Capriccio sopra la lontananza* and *Denn du wirst meine Seele* probably written.		Battle of Blenheim. Newton's *Opticks*.
1705	Hears Buxtehude in Lübeck.	Handel's first opera: *Almira*.	Leibniz: *New Essays on Human Understanding*.
1706		Handel in Italy (to 1709).	Emperor Leopold I dies; succeeded by Joseph I. Charles XII of Sweden occupies Saxony.
1707	Organist at Blasiuskirche, Mühlhausen. Marries Maria Barbara Bach (23). Toccata in D minor.	Death of Buxtehude (70).	
1708	*Gott ist mein König* written. Organist and court musician to Duke Wilhelm Ernst at Weimar. First child, Catharina Dorothea, born.	Torelli: *Concerti grossi*, op. 8.	Battle of Oudenaarde.
1708–23	Organ chorales, including Leipzig chorales; organ preludes and fugues.		

DATE	LIFE AND WORKS	MUSICAL CONTEXT	HISTORICAL BACKGROUND
1709		Death of Torelli (51).	Charles XII defeated by Peter the Great at Poltava.
1710	Wilhelm Friedemann, second child, born.	Handel court conductor at Hanover. Birth of Pergolesi.	Leibniz: *Theodicy.* Thomasius: *Short Outline of Political Prudence.*
1711		Handel settles in London. Vivaldi: *L'estro armonico,* op. 3.	Death of Austrian Emperor Joseph I: accession of Charles VI. Publication of *Spectator* (England).
1713	Clavier arrangements of concertos by Vivaldi. Most of *Orgel-Büchlein* (to 1716). Brandenburg Concertos (to 1721).	Death of Corelli (60). F. Couperin: *Pièces de Clavecin* I.	Treaty of Utrecht. Pragmatic Sanction issued. Death of Frederick I; accession of Frederick William I of Prussia.
1714	Promoted to Konzertmeister at Weimar. Carl Philipp Emanuel born.	Birth of Gluck. Vivaldi: *La stravaganza,* op. 4.	Accession of George I (elector of Hanover) as king of Great Britain.
1715	Johann Gottfried Bernhard born. English Suites.		Death of Louis XIV: duc d'Orléans regent. Jacobite Rebellion.
1717	Kapellmeister to Prince Leopold of Anhalt-Cöthen (leaves Weimar, Dec.). 6 sonatas for violin and harpsichord; orchestral suites 1 and 4; 3 violin concertos; concerto for 2 violins; flute sonatas in A, b, C and e (to 1723).	Handel: *Water Music.* F. Couperin: *Pièces de Clavecin* II.	Peter the Great visits Paris. J. J. Winckelmann born. Freemasons founded (England).
1718	Visits Carlsbad with Leopold, May–June.	Handel: *Acis and Galatea.*	Charles XII of Sweden dies.
1719		L. Mozart born.	Defoe: *Robinson Crusoe.*
1720	Begins clavier book for WF. Wife dies. 3 sonatas and 3 partitas for solo violin; 6 cello suites and Chromatic Fantasia and Fugue.		South Sea Bubble (Great Britain). Mississippi Bubble: collapse of Law's financial schemes (France).
1721	Brandenburg Concertos dedicated to Margrave. Marries Anna Magdalena Wilcke (20) 3 Dec. Marriage of Prince Leopold.		Walpole First Lord of the Treasury 1721–42 (Great Britain).
1722	*Well-tempered Clavier* I; 6 French Suites.	Rameau: *Treatise on Harmony.* F. Couperin: *Pièces de Clavecin* III.	
1723	Thomaskantor, Leipzig. Cantata 75 performed in Nikolaikirche, 30 May. E flat Magnificat performed in Thomaskirche, 25 Dec.		General Directory established in Prussia. Louis XV attains his majority.
1723–6	15 two-part and 15 three-part Inventions; bulk of church cantatas.		
1724	*St John Passion* performed in Nikolaikirche.		Birth of Kant. Death of Peter the Great.
1725	*Easter Oratorio.* Anna Magdalena's *Clavierbüchlein* II.	Vivaldi: *The Four Seasons.*	
1726	Elisabeth Juliana Friederika (11th child) born. Partita I published.	F. Couperin: *Les Nations.*	Swift: *Gulliver's Travels.*
1727	Possible first performance of *St Matthew Passion* in Thomaskirche. *Trauer Ode* performed. 6 trio sonatas for organ probably composed.	Handel: *Coronation Anthems.*	Accession of George II (Great Britain). Death of Newton (85).

DATE	LIFE AND WORKS	MUSICAL CONTEXT	HISTORICAL BACKGROUND
1728	Prince Leopold (33) dies, 19 Nov. *Magnificat* in D (to 1731).		Foreign Ministry (*Kabinetsministerium*) established in Prussia. Gay: *The Beggar's Opera*.
1729	Performs funeral music for Prince Leopold at Cöthen. *St Matthew Passion* (first?) performed (15 April). Assumes direction of collegium musicum. Illness prevents meeting with Handel.	Pergolesi: *Stabat Mater*. D. Scarlatti moves to Spain.	
1729–40	Orchestral suites 2 and 3.		
1730	Bach's memorandum on church music to town council. J. M. Gesner Rector of Thomasschule. Flute, violin and harpsichord concerto.	F. Couperin: *Pièces de Clavecin* IV.	Gottsched: *Essay towards a Critical Poetic Art for the Germans*.
1731	*Clavier-Übung* I published. *St Mark Passion* performed in Thomaskirche.		20,000 Protestants expelled from Salzburg.
1732		Birth of Haydn.	Pope: *Essay on Man* (to 1734).
1733	WF (23) organist at Sophienkirche, Dresden, June. JSB presents *Missa* (BWV232) to elector of Saxony.	Rameau: *Hippolyte et Aricie*. Pergolesi: *La serva padrona*. Death of F. Couperin (65) and G. Böhm (72).	Holbach: *Système social*. Death of elector of Saxony, also Augustus II of Poland. War of the Polish succession (to 1735).
1734	J. A. Ernesti Thomasschule Rector. *Christmas Oratorio* performed Christmas / New Year 1734–5.		
1735	18th child, Johann Christian, born. *Clavier-Übung* II (Italian Concerto and French Overture in b) published.	Rameau: *Les Indes galantes*.	Linnaeus: *Systema Naturae*. Augustus III confirmed as Polish king.
1736	Battle with Ernesti begins. Appointed Hofcompositeur to elector of Saxony.	Death of Pergolesi.	Voltaire begins to correspond with Frederick of Prussia.
1737	Scheibe publishes adverse criticism of JSB.	Rameau: *Castor et Pollux*.	Göttingen University founded.
1738	CPE (24) in service of Crown Prince Frederick of Prussia. *Well-tempered Clavier* II (to 1742).	Handel: Organ Concertos, op. 4.	
1739	JGB dies. *Clavier-Übung* III published.	Handel: *Israel in Egypt*.	
1740		Handel: *Concerti grossi*, op. 12.	Frederick II (the 'Great') becomes king of Prussia (to 1786); invades Silesia. Death of Emperor Charles VI; Maria Theresa empress of Austria. War of Austrian Succession (to 1748).
1741	Anna Magdalena seriously ill. *Clavier-Übung* IV (Goldberg Variations) published (to 1742).	Death of Vivaldi. Gluck: *Artaserse*. Handel: *Deidamia*.	Prussian army defeats Austrians at Mollowitz. Franco-Prussian alliance.
1742	20th and last child – Regina Susanna – born.	Handel: *Messiah*.	Charles Albert of Bavaria elected Holy Roman Emperor.
1744	CPE marries in Berlin.		Battle of Dettingen. Frederick II takes Prague. Second Silesian War.
1745	Writing the *Art of Fugue* (to 1750; pub. 1751).		Jacobite Rebellion under 'Bonnie Prince Charlie'. Peace of Dresden (Prussia and Austria). Election of Francis I, husband of Maria Theresa, as Holy Roman Emperor.

DATE	LIFE AND WORKS	MUSICAL CONTEXT	HISTORICAL BACKGROUND
1746	WF organist at the Liebfrauenkirche, Halle.		Death of Philip V of Spain; succeeded by Ferdinand VI.
			Diderot: *Pensées philosophiques.*
1747	Visits Frederick the Great's court at Potsdam, 7–8 May. Gives organ recital in Heiliggeistkirche, 8 May. *Musical Offering* published. Joins Society of Musical Sciences, June, for which he writes the Canonic Variations. First grandchild, Anna Carolina Philippina, born Sept.		First *Realschule* founded in Berlin by Johann Hecker. Orangist revolution in United Provinces. Voltaire: *Zadig.*
1748	*Vom Himmel hoch* (Canonic Variations) published.		Treaty of Aix-la-Chapelle. Klopstock: *Messias.* Montesquieu: *De l'esprit des lois.* Fielding: *Tom Jones.* Pompeii excavated.
1749	Daughter Elisabeth marries J. C. Altnikol in Leipzig. Harrer performs *Probe*, 8 June, as Bach's probable successor.	Handel: *Music for the Royal Fireworks.*	Birth of Goethe. Hume: *Enquiry concerning Human Understanding.*
1750	JCF (18) court musician at Bückeburg, Jan. *Art of Fugue* engraved. JSB operated on by oculist John Taylor. Dies 28 July. Buried in graveyard of Johanniskirche, 31 July.		
1751	*Art of Fugue* published.	Geminiani: *Art of Playing on the Violin.*	
1752		*Guerre des Bouffons* in France between supporters of French and Italian music.	Voltaire: *Micromégas.*
1756		Birth of Mozart.	Lisbon earthquake. Beginning of Seven Years' War.
1757		Death of D. Scarlatti.	
1758–60		Haydn's first five symphonies.	
1759		Death of Handel.	Voltaire: *Candide.*

Index

Page numbers in *italics* refer to illustrations

Acknowledgements

The Publishers gratefully acknowledge permission given by the following to reproduce illustrations and photographs: Staatsbibliothek zu Berlin – Preussischer Kulturbesitz, Musikabteilung mit Mendelssohn-Archiv 4, 16, 58, 75, 126, 139, 149, 157; AKG London 5, 19 (Deutsche Staatsbibliothek), 20, 31, 32, 36, 52, 54 (Angermuseum, Erfurt), 63, 65 (Bachhaus, Eisenach), 69, 73, 80, 83, 84, 86, 90, 93 & 105 (Museum für Kunst und Gewerbe, Hamburg), 99, 115 (Liceo Musicale, Bologna), 121, 123 (Nationalgalerie Preussischer Kulturbesitz, Berlin), 131, 150 (Stadtgeschichtliches Museum, Leipzig), 152, 154 (Musée du Louvre, Paris), 164; Photo © Gloria Lunel, Milan 8; © Photo RMN – G. Blot/ C. Jean (Versailles et Trianon) 14; Museum für das Fürstentum, Lüneburg 28; Bomann-Museum, Celle, 29; Bibliothek der Hansestadt, Lübeck/photo Margaret Witzke 37; Stadtarchiv, Mühlhausen 40; Glasgow University Library, Department of Special Collections 41, 138; Bildarchiv Preussischer Kulturbesitz, Berlin 46, 51; Kunstsammlungen zu Weimar/Photo Dressler 47; Royal College of Music, London 50, 74; © Collection VIOLLET 55; Bach-Archiv Leipzig 60; Bayerisches Nationalmuseum 70; from *Unfehlbare Engel-Freude Gesang-Buch*, Leipzig (1710) 79; Stadtgeschichtliches Museum, Leipzig 87; Bachhaus, Eisenach 88; Stadtarchiv, Leipzig 89; Stadtbibliothek Leipzig, Rep. III, fol 15e, on deposit at the Bach-Archiv Leipzig 100; Bildarchiv der Österreichischen Nationalbibliothek, Vienna 124; Schloss- und Spielkartenmuseum, Altenburg 132; Photo Ullstein 144; from J. G. Puschner, *Neue und Curieuse Theatralische Tantz-Schule*, Nuremburg (1716) 144; Hulton Getty 145. Map relief (p. vi): Mountain High Maps © 1995 Digital Wisdom, Inc.

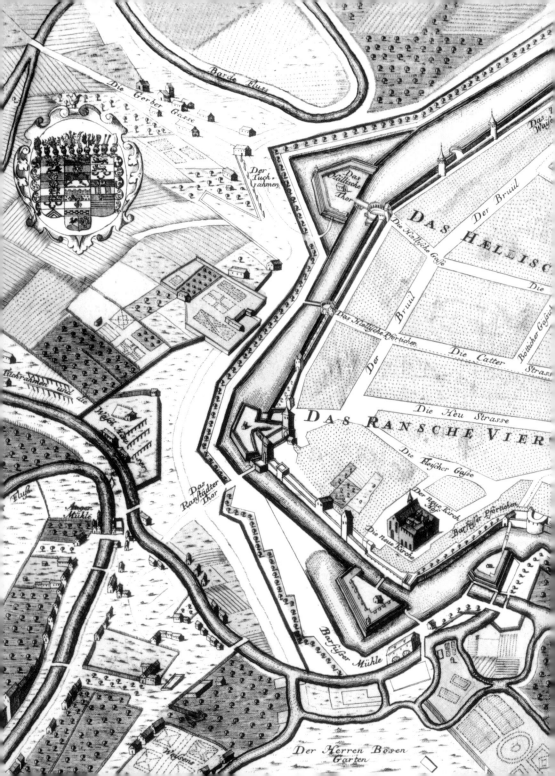

Die Gerber Gasse

Barde Fluss

Der Tuch Rahmen

Das Hällische Thor

Das Weise

Der Bruul

DAS HÆLLISCH

Die Hällische Gasse

Das Hällische Pförtchen

Der Bruul

Die Catter Strasse

Böttcher Grabicht

Die

Die Heu Strasse

DAS RANSCHE VIER

Tuchrahmen und die

Welsch Tor

Flyss

Anger Mühle

Das Ranstädter Thor

Die Fleischer Gasse

Der neue Kirch Hof

Die Neue Kirch

Barfüsser Pförtchen

Barfüser Mühle

Der Herren Bösen Garten

Welse